HOW TO
GROW
GREAT
KIDS

D0756020

# HOW TO GROW GREAT KIDS

## THE GOOD PARENTS GUIDE TO REARING SOCIABLE, CONFIDENT AND HEALTHY CHILDREN.

ALLISON LEE

howtobooks

The paper used for this book is FSC certified and totally chlorine free. FSC (The Forest Stewardship Council) is an international network to promote responsible management of the world's forests.



Published by How To Books Ltd
Spring Hill House, Spring Hill Road
Begbroke, Oxford OX5 1RX, United Kingdom
Tel: (01865) 375794, Fax: (01865) 379162

How To Books greatly reduce the carbon footprint of their books by sourcing their typesetting and printing in the UK.



British Library Cataloguing in Publication Data
A catalogue record for this book is available from the British Library

ISBN 978 1 84528 288 2

Cover design by Baseline Arts Ltd, Oxford
Produced for How To Books by Deer Park Productions, Tavistock
Typeset by Kestrel Data, Exeter, Devon
Printed and bound by Cromwell Press Group, Trowbridge, Wiltshire

# Contents


Acknowledgements xiii

Introduction xv

## Part One: How to grow confident, sociable kids

**1 Family values** **3**

How family life has changed in recent years 3
Being a good role model 3
Working parents 4
Coping with pressures and responsibilities 6

**2 What kind of parent are you?** **8**

Parenting styles 8
How do you control your behaviour? 11
What kind of relationship do you have with your child? 14
What kind of relationship would you like with your child? 15
Viewing parenting as a partnership 17
Parenting alone 19

**3 Factors influencing children's behaviour** **21**

Family structure 21
Diet 24
Divorce and separation 29
Death 32
Siblings 32
Illness 34
Culture 34
Moving house or school 35

Unemployment 35
Disability 36
Gender 36

**4 Why do I need to manage my child's behaviour? 37**

Why does my child misbehave? 37
Reasons for misbehaving 38
How children learn about behaviour 43
Adapting your parenting approach to each child 45

**5 Behaviour inside the home 47**

Keeping one set of rules 47
Being consistent 48
Showing respect 48
Setting boundaries 51

**6 Behaviour outside the home 54**

Social acceptance 54
Behaving appropriately in public 56
Temper tantrums 60

**7 Encouraging positive behaviour 62**

Building a framework 62
Understanding what motivates young children 65
Empowerment 67
Using rewards to reinforce positive behaviour 69

**8 Responding to unwanted behaviour 71**

What triggers unwanted behaviour? 71
Dealing with unwanted behaviour 72
Smacking 72
Shouting 74
Using body language 75
Applying punishments and sanctions 76

**9 Exploring feelings** **82**

Understanding how your child is feeling 82
Showing feelings and emotions 85
Raising a child's self-esteem 87
Encouraging self-respect in children 89
Giving a child responsibility 90
Acknowledging your child's individuality 91

**10 Social skills** **92**

How friendships are formed 92
Different stages of play 93
Changing friendships 95
Popularity 95
Working together 97
When children fall out 99
Controlling emotions 100
Shyness 103

**11 Tackling bullies** **106**

What is bullying? 106
The bully 107
Is your child a bully? 108
The victim 112
Recognising bullying 113
Understanding bullying 115
Dealing with incidents of bullying 116
Moving your child to another school 119
Bullying outside school 120

**Part Two: How to grow healthy kids**

**12 The principles of nutrition** **125**

Providing a healthy diet for children 125
The food pyramid 125
Key nutrients 126
Macronutrients 127
Micronutrients 130

Non-nutrients 134
Encouraging healthy eating and food choices 136

**13 The principles of fitness 141**

Getting children physically fit 141
Avoiding 'couch potatoes' 141
Benefits of physical exercise 142
Ways to get children active 143
Staying fit for life 147

**14 Meal planning 150**

Breakfast – the right start to the day 150
Shopping for the right foods 152
Pleasing everyone 155

**15 Safety in the kitchen 157**

Ensuring your kitchen is hygienic 157
Food safety 157
Storing food 159
Preparing food 160
Cooking food 161
Food poisoning 161
Effective hand washing 163

**16 Your child during their first year 165**

A good start to healthy eating 165
Vital nutrition for babies 165
Breast-feeding 166
Bottle-feeding 167
Weaning 169
The overweight baby 172
Finger food 173

**17 Your child aged one to three years 175**

Growth rate and calorie intake 175
Fussy eaters 176

Vital nutrition for toddlers 176
Keeping your toddler active 178

**18 Your child aged three to five years 182**

Vital nutrition for pre-school children 182
Meal-time battles 182
Adequate diet for a pre-school child 183
Keeping your pre-school child active 183

**19 Your child aged six to twelve years 188**

Vital nutrition for school-aged children 188
Keeping your school-aged child active 190

**20 Your teenager 192**

Adolescence 192
Vital nutrition for your teenager 192
Freedom of choice 194
Keeping teenagers active 194
Body image 196

**21 Food allergies and intolerances 202**

Common allergies 202
Preventing allergies 204
Milk allergies 204
Wheat allergies 206
Egg allergies 206

**22 Nutrition through illness 209**

The importance of adequate nutrition 209
Feeding a child who is ill 210
Dealing with vomiting and diarrhoea 212
Dehydration 212

**23 Unhealthy foods** 216
Additives 216
Too much sugar 218
Too much salt 219
Fatty foods 221
Fizzy drinks 222
Takeaways 222

**24 Snacking** 225
Eating between meals 225
Foods to avoid snacking on 228
Healthy foods for snacks 228

**25 Overweight children** 230
Body Mass Index 230
What to do if your child is overweight 233

**26 Fussy eaters** 235
Being a good role model 235
Building up an appetite 237
Strategies for dealing with fussy eaters 238

**27 Organic food v conventional food** 241
What's in the food we eat? 241
Are organic foods worth the extra cost? 242
Growing your own 242

**28 School meals or packed lunches?** 244
Are school meals healthy? 244
New nutritional standards 245
School meal guidelines 245
What can parents do to ensure a healthy school lunch? 247
Encouraging children to choose healthier options 248
Providing your child with a healthy lunchbox 249

Lunchbox contents 250
The perfect lunchbox 254

**29 Five a day 255**

Why is it important that children get their 'five a day'? 255
How much is a portion? 255
Achieving five a day 256
Encouraging your child to eat more fruit and vegetables 257

**30 Vegetarian diets 262**

The vegetarian diet 262
Types of vegetarian diet 262
How does a vegetarian diet affect health? 263
Should children be given a vegetarian diet? 263
What the body needs 264
Ensuring your vegetarian child eats healthily 264

**31 Recipes for children 269**

Babies up to 12 months 269
Toddlers one to three years 272
Pre-school children three to five years 273
School-age children five to 12 years 274
Teenagers 275
Family meals 277

Useful telephone numbers and websites 279

Index 281

# Acknowledgements

Being a parent has undoubtedly been one of the most rewarding and challenging aspects of my life. If anyone tells you that it is easy to get children to eat a healthy balanced diet and remain active I would say they are kidding you! There is not, and never will be, a quick fix however, what I would say is that children copy their parents attitudes to life and therefore the onus is on us to help our children to lead a fit, active and healthy lifestyle.

I would like to thank Nikki Read and Giles Lewis for giving me the opportunity of having another book published through How to Books.

My thanks also go to my own parents Roger and Cynthia Fahey for providing me with a memorable childhood, and for encouraging me to lead a healthy lifestyle and enabling me to pass this on to my own children Sam and David. Thanks as always goes to my husband for sharing the trials and tribulations having children has brought.

# Introduction

As parents we all want the best for our children. We want them to be healthy and active, do well at school, pass examinations, get a good job, have lots of friends and be happy and fulfilled.

Nothing can prepare you for being a parent. Children can and do push the boundaries and often test your nerves, emotions and sanity into the bargain. As your child goes through the various stages and transitions associated with growing up you will be faced with yet more dilemmas and anxieties. However one thing is certain, no matter how far your children push you and how tempted you are to throw in the towel you cannot give up. Your child is here to stay. He or she is not a toy which can be thrown into the cupboard when you become bored, so perseverance is a must when being a parent!

Parenting is the most difficult but rewarding job known to mankind. It is poorly paid but the rewards are clear for all to see when your child grows and develops into a thriving, kind, considerate human being and you can pat yourself on the back for having done a good job!

Millions of people have been parents before you and millions more will follow in your footsteps. Parenting is mostly trial and error but the wise parents understand the importance of providing their children with a healthy balanced diet in order for them to maintain a fit and active lifestyle along with the love, space, time and resources they require in order for them to explore their feelings, manage their behaviour in an acceptable manner, relate to others and develop meaningful relationships.

The trick to successful parenting is to find the right balance for your own family and to bring your children up in a way which you are comfortable with.

This book covers all aspects of bringing up children including development, diet and exercise and it offers sensitive, practical advice including information about parenting in general, exercise and dietary needs.

I hope this book will provide you with reassurance of your own capabilities whilst offering alternative suggestions if needed.

# Part One

## How to Grow Confident, Sociable Kids

Part One will help you to:

- Encourage your child's social and self-help skills
- Manage your child's behaviour successfully
- Promote your child's emotional wellbeing.

# Family Values

## How family life has changed in recent years

Some would say that families today are almost unrecognisable compared to say, 50 years ago; others would argue that much of the basics of family life remain the same. What is certain is that family life, the world over, is changing shape to some degree as we alter the way we live, work and bring up our children.

Family life is certainly much busier and more stressful today than it was a decade or more ago with many parents struggling to balance work and family life. Parenting is often a subject of intense debate with some arguing that a mother's place is at home with her children whilst others consider that women have the right to a worthwhile career as well as being a parent.

## Being a good role model

Family life may well have changed but family *values* remain as strong today as they ever were. All parents want their children to grow up happy and healthy and to possess the skills necessary for them to become valued and accepted members of society. However, in order to do this, children need to know how to be confident, sociable and well behaved. These skills need to be taught as they do not come naturally! A good role model is therefore vital. Teaching children how to behave in an acceptable manner is a complex procedure and one which can often be very daunting for parents.

## Teaching your child right from wrong

Parents can, and indeed do, make an enormous difference to their child's chances of success in life and it is vital that they understand just how important a role they play.

In the past children were expected to 'be seen and not heard', they knew their place and they were often punished, physically, for misbehaving. Many would argue that children in the past knew how to behave in comparison to today's children who are often perceived as being spoilt, lazy and uncooperative. I doubt many parents, however, would like to go back to the days where children were expected to sit silently and possess no ideas or views. Children, as we know, are a great source of enjoyment particularly to their parents, however it is important that they understand the 'rules' of society and that they learn how to respect others in order to gain respect for themselves.

# Working parents

Parents go out to work for all sorts of reasons. Their need to work may be dictated by:

- finances
- career prospects
- a desire for adult company.

Life is all about compromise and choice and it is important to remember that everyone has different reasons for wanting or needing to work.

Most working parents will share some common emotions such as:

- guilt at enjoying their job
- guilt at leaving their children

- feeling robbed of the time they can spend with their children
- tiredness
- frustration.

Talk to any parent and you probably won't be surprised to find that all of them share some form of guilt. Those who stay at home to look after their children feel guilty because they don't have a career or contribute to the family finances; those who go out to work feel guilty because they are not at home looking after their children.

## Over compensating

It is *very* important that working parents do not fall into the trap of 'over compensating' for their absence through work by allowing their child too much freedom, as this will ultimately lead to a lack of discipline and proper parental control. That is not to say that parents should be ruthless disciplinarians it just means you need to bear in mind that children will not benefit from relaxed rules in place of quality time with their parents.

## Enjoying quality time with your child

The all important, often discussed 'quality time' means taking the time to listen to, interact with and respond to your child in an unhurried manner. Quality time means that your child has your undivided attention for some part of the day. This may be sitting having a leisurely dinner around the table when you are able to listen to what your child has done at nursery, school or with their childminder; it may be playing in the bath with them or when reading a bedtime story. You need to be able to concentrate completely on your child and what they are saying without any other distractions.

In order to make quality time special and important you need to take several things into consideration:

- You will be tired after a busy day at work and so too will your child, therefore the amount of quality time you spend together at the end of a working day may be limited.
- Your child will have spent most of the day away from you, so it is perfectly natural that they will demand your attention.
- You will probably still have household chores to do such as the washing, ironing and preparing a meal, so you will need to be organised and plan in advance if everything is to get done.

Stay-at-home mums also need to look closely at the amount of quality time they spend with their children. They may be with their children 24 hours a day but how much of this time is actually spent talking to and interacting with their offspring and how much time is spent washing, ironing, cooking and cleaning?

## Coping with pressures and responsibilities

All parents, regardless of whether they work or stay at home with their children, will face pressure and stress at some point in their lives due to the responsibilities that child rearing entails.

In general terms the pressures and stresses faced by today's parents may involve one or more of the following:

- Coping as a single parent
- Coping with caring for several children
- Coping with a baby who does not sleep
- Coping with a baby who cries constantly
- Living away from family and friends and therefore having a limited support network
- Employment problems
- Financial problems

- Drug or alcohol problems
- Relationship difficulties
- Coping with a child who has a disability or ill health
- Suffering from a disability or ill health yourself
- Being a very young or inexperienced parent.

Some people under pressure may be able to cope quite admirably most of the time. Others may react altogether differently under such stresses and, if other factors such as exhaustion, worry, low self-esteem, guilt or depression are added to the responsibilities, it is not surprising that some parents find family life difficult to cope with.

## Accepting imperfection

If the truth were really known would children actually want their parents to be able to cope with everything, to know all the answers and never put a foot wrong? Of course not! They would have an impossible role model to follow and they would end up feeling as if *they* had failed miserably trying to achieve the impossible.

Although parents should be aware of the pressures and stresses of everyday life and should strive, where possible, to improve their parenting skills, they also need to remember that parenting should be fun. Enjoy your children. Don't set your standards too high and you won't feel as though you are a terrible failure if you snatch two hours' sleep in the afternoon because you have been awake all night with a crying baby. Will anyone really notice whether you have vacuumed the living room carpet that day? Let your common sense prevail and use your time sensibly.

# 2 What kind of parent are you?

## Parenting styles

We all have our own shortcomings and foibles and just as every child is unique so too is every parent. What works well for some families may prove disastrous for others, therefore we need to understand that there are no 'right' or 'wrong' ways to bring up children.

Babies are not programmed 'good', 'bad' or 'workable'. It is up to you, as a parent, to teach your child right from wrong, good from bad and instil in them values and respect. How you do this will very much depend on your personal *parenting style*. You may be a laid-back kind of person with very few rules, and the rules you do have may be flexible; or you may be a very strict parent with unbending rules that you expect your child to adhere to at all times. On the other hand, and this is by far the best kind of parenting style to adopt, you could be somewhere between the two; certain of how you expect your children to behave but making allowances along the way for the fact that, like you, no one is perfect and we all make mistakes some time.

These three styles of parenting are commonly known as:

- Permissive
- Authoritarian
- Authoritative.

## Permissive parenting

This kind of parenting is actually becoming more and more popular as a result of modern attitudes to children. The common view is that children should have a say in the way they lead their lives and, to some extent, this is favourable. However, it is when the permissive parenting style adopts a 'couldn't care less' or 'let them get on with it' attitude when the problems will begin to surface.

### *Providing limits and boundaries*

All children need limits and boundaries in order to feel safe and secure and sometimes the lack of structure present in the permissive style of parenting can cause confusion for the children and chaos for the family.

The advantages to a permissive style of parenting are:

- Flexibility
- Close and loving relationships between parent and child
- Minimal confrontation as the child is usually allowed what they want
- Freedom given to the child to learn how to manage their own behaviour
- No opportunity for the child to be punished physically
- No verbal reprimands or shouting
- Inclusion of the child in discussions about behaviour.

The disadvantages to a permissive style of parenting are:

- The child may find it difficult to work within boundaries
- The child may not understand what is and is not allowed
- The child may expect to 'get away' with inappropriate behaviour when outside the home.

## Authoritarian parenting

Often referred to as a 'Victorian' approach to parenting, authoritarian parents are old-fashioned in their approach to bringing up children. They often hold the belief that children today are given too much freedom and, as a result, lack values and respect.

Authoritarian parents have fixed routines and rules which they expect their children to abide by.

The advantages to an authoritarian style of parenting are:

- The child will find working within boundaries easy
- The child will have a clear view of what is and is not acceptable behaviour
- The child will feel safe and secure
- The child will find adjusting to settings outside the home easy.

The disadvantages to an authoritarian style of parenting are:

- There may be a lot of confrontations between the child and parent
- The parent may resort to physical violence
- The parent may resort to shouting
- The child may feel trapped
- The child may feel bullied
- The child may rebel at a later stage
- The child may have little opportunity to express themselves
- There is little room for flexibility.

## Authoritative parenting

A mix of permissive and authoritarian styles of parenting, authoritative parents are capable of allowing their child the freedom to 'be themselves' whilst retaining the overall say in how things are done. Although authoritative parents lay down rules and set boundaries they take the time to explain these rules and boundaries and to listen to their children. They have realistic views of what their child is likely to achieve and take a firm but fair attitude.

The advantages to an authoritative style of parenting are:

- The child has clear and consistent rules and boundaries
- The child has a good understanding of what is expected of them
- The relationship between the parent and child is often one based on love, trust and mutual respect.

The disadvantages to an authoritative style of parenting are:

- It can, at times, be difficult to find and maintain a balance
- Despite a positive approach, children may still feel hard done by particularly if their friends' parents are more permissive.

# How do you control your behaviour?

Before we can begin to look at ways of understanding why children behave in certain ways and what we can do to effectively manage their behaviour it is perhaps important to take a closer look at our own behaviour. We need to determine what triggers the way we feel and how we respond to certain situations. By doing this we can gain an insight into what makes our children tick and hopefully see where our own behaviour is mirrored or copied by them.

Remember, children do not just copy the positive traits they see in their parents; they can, and often do, copy the negative sides to their behaviour as well.

Behaviour is always better taught well the first time around rather than trying to undo the bad and trying to re-educate the child. Positive role models in the form of loving, respectful parents are therefore essential if children are to learn how to behave well.

## Influences on your parenting style

There are several influences which may affect the sort of parent you are and these include:

- The way you have been brought up
- The type of person you are and what you expect from your children
- The type of children you have.

### *The way you have been brought up*

Most of us are strongly influenced by our own parents' beliefs and the way in which we were raised ourselves and we often repeat the cycle, regardless of whether our own upbringing was a positive one or not. Breaking the cycle of a poor upbringing can be very difficult as we tend to fall into a pattern and, even if you thought your own upbringing was too strict or severe, you may well find yourself mirroring this kind of upbringing for your own children. This can be because you do not know any other way of being a parent or because subconsciously you believe this to be the correct way of parenting.

Some parents, however, will bring their own children up in the completely opposite way. If they felt their own upbringing was too strict, for example, they may adopt a permissive style of parenting themselves and allow their children the freedom they felt they were deprived of.

### *The type of person you are and what you expect from your children*

Your own beliefs and traits will go a long way towards shaping how you act as a parent and what you expect from your own children. You may be a well-organised person who likes a structure to their life and, as such, you are more likely to want control over your children and family life. On the other hand, you may be laid back and relaxed, and feel content allowing your children to have lots of freedom. You may have been brought up in a strict environment yourself where you were not allowed to misbehave and, as a result, you will probably expect your own children to behave in much the same way.

### *The type of children you have*

You may be very fortunate and have children who instinctively know how to behave – though this is *very* rare – who only need reminding occasionally that their behaviour is unacceptable. Or you may have children who appear to push the boundaries to the limit at every given opportunity and need constantly reminding about how to behave.

You may have two or more children but they will all be different. Avoid comparing your children or saying things like 'Why can't you be more like your brother/sister?', as this will undermine their individuality and cause resentment between siblings. Shy, timid children will need a different style of parenting to loud, boisterous and confident children.

## Controlling your temper

Controlling your own behaviour, and in particular your temper, is absolutely crucial when bringing up children. 'Do as I say and not as I do' is a very old-fashioned and, dare I say it, unacceptable saying for parents to use as an excuse when their children copy their own undesirable behaviour. If you lose your temper, rant and rave and throw things around the house when things don't go in your favour is it really any wonder that your child has temper tantrums?

### Providing a positive role model

Once again, providing your child with a positive role model is crucial. Show your child that situations can be resolved in an amicable, controlled manner with no need for anger and aggression, and they are much more likely to resort to this kind of behaviour themselves. Allow them to witness you swearing and shouting when things don't go according to plan and they will be well on their way to becoming little monsters before they reach primary school.

## What kind of relationship do you have with your child?

This must really be the million dollar question! What kind of relationship do you have with your child? We may know what kind of relationship we would *like* to have with our child but this, of course, is not the same as admitting what we *actually* have.

If you would like a close and intimate relationship with your child where you share secrets, clothes and makeup but you are a mother to a 15 year old boy you may have to rethink your ideas slightly!

### Allowing your child to be themselves

Even mothers of daughters may not achieve the closeness they would like. If the daughter is independent and headstrong it is highly unlikely they will endure shopping trips with their mothers when they prefer to hang out with their friends. The trick is to allow your child to be themselves. Let them know, from a very early age, that you are there for them when they need you and refrain from becoming dependent on them.

### Responding to your child

To be able to answer the all important question of 'What kind of relationship do I have with my child?', you need to explore your relationship and think carefully about how you respond to your child when:

- they are misbehaving
- they are behaving well.

It is easy to overlook the child who is playing quietly and who does as they are told, but is it really fair for the child who misbehaves to get more attention than those who don't?

The relationship you have with your child will depend as much on how you respond to them on an everyday level as well as how you discipline them. You may well have to chastise your child from time to time if they are misbehaving. If you also show them love and affection and spend time with them, helping them, teaching them and nurturing them, they will know how much they are loved and cherished even if you are cross with them occasionally.

## What kind of relationship would you like with your child?

The kind of relationship you have with your child and the kind you would like may, at times, seem poles apart. However it is important to persevere and keep striving for the things you consider important. Parenting is a long process, often tiring and sometimes overwhelming, but the joys far outweigh the disappointments, if you set your goals and keep your priorities in the forefront of your mind when things get tough.

Most parents, if asked what kind of a relationship they would like with their child, would include some or all of the descriptions below:

- loving
- close
- respectful
- affectionate
- tender

- friendly
- equal.

Some may answer in a completely opposite manner and include the following:

- strict
- controlled
- distant
- disciplined.

## Your child's perspective

Although you may like to think that you have the kind of relationship with your child which includes some or all of the descriptions in the first category it is unlikely, if asked, that your child will see things this way. Chances are your child will describe the relationship they have with you as strict, controlled, distant and disciplined.

## Listing your priorities

All parents will, and should, have certain priorities which they consider essential when parenting their children. It is important to look at your own list of priorities and to keep these in mind at all times when making decisions that will affect your child.

Your priorities may include:

- Having a fun and carefree time with your children to ensure that their childhood is happy and free from stress and worry
- Ensuring that your children feel loved and valued
- Ensuring that your children feel safe and secure

- Helping your children to achieve academic success
- Helping your children to achieve emotional success
- Teaching your children right from wrong and instilling a good ethical understanding
- Teaching your children how to behave well
- Spending quality time with each of your children both together and separately.

You may, however, pay little heed to these kinds of priorities and have the following high on your agenda:

- Keeping the house clean and tidy
- Keeping the children clean
- Ensuring that the washing and ironing is done regularly.

Other priorities you may consider important might include:

- Preparing healthy, nutritional meals
- Making time for yourself
- Making time for your husband or partner
- Keeping on top of your work commitments.

## Viewing parenting as a partnership

Whenever we think of children and the everyday life of the family – the discipline, the treats, the shopping, the cooking, the planning of outings and activities, the housework, the washing and the ironing – most of us conjure up an image of a harassed mother rushing around after her children, exhaustedly trying to keep things together. How many of us think of the father in place of the mother? In today's society when a great number of mothers work full time, family life must be viewed as a partnership in *every* sense of the word.

## A father's role

Fathers have an equal responsibility towards their children and the smooth running of the home. Many women work equal, and sometimes longer, hours than their partners. It is therefore unacceptable for men to come home from work and wait for their partners to get home an hour later to cook them a meal. The extra income earned by women is a huge bonus in many households today and I believe fathers actually enjoy the hands on participation of family life. Whereas at one time they may have been restricted to spending half an hour with their children before bedtime fathers now have the chance to spend time with their children without feeling as though it is 'women's work'.

## United decision making

A lot of parents fall into the trap of telling their children to ask their mum/dad if they wish to avoid saying 'no' to a request and this method of passing the buck should be avoided as it makes the other parent appear mean if they say no to the child's request. It is far better to say 'I will talk to your mum/dad about that and let you know.' That way your child can be sure that *both* parents have given their request some thought before coming to an answer. The child is much less likely to question your decision if they know that it is a joint one and that you are both in total agreement.

Parenting is not a competition for love and affection and parents should avoid scoring points over one another at all costs. Many mothers have been known to chastise a child who is misbehaving with 'just you wait until your father gets home'. This threat tells the child that they have to fear their father's wrath because their mother can not deal with their behaviour. It also puts the father in the difficult situation of having to respond to behaviour they have not witnessed and which could have occurred hours before and the child has forgotten about, in order to appease the irate and harassed mother.

## Sending mixed messages

Although having the support of a partner can be reassuring it can also bring with it added complications. Having another adult in the house can be advantageous when parenting begins to take its toll providing you do not take out your stresses and anxieties on each other. It can be very daunting when you are presented with a newborn baby; the worry of caring for a young child, who is completely and utterly dependent on you 24 hours a day, can leave you with little time for each other. It is important that you pull together during this time and support each other through any difficulties.

## Parenting alone

Parenting as a partnership need not necessarily mean that the mother and father have to be members of the team. Although children are often brought up by just one parent, other people can be involved in helping to bring them up. Parents may enlist the help of other family members, friends and, in many cases, where both parents go out to work, parents increasingly rely on nannies and childminders to help with the care of their children. This important network of people, along with nursery staff and teachers, is vital for the continued care and education of children today.

If you find yourself without a partner to help you to bring up your child, the chances are that the stress and worry will be even greater with no one to share the anxiety with. On the upside, neither will you have anyone else to think about except yourself and your baby.

Although being a single parent means shouldering all the responsibilities yourself, this can have its advantages. It will be much easier for you to be consistent with your child's upbringing as there will be no conflicting ideas and opinions to take into account. The final decisions and choices about what your child is and isn't allowed to do will ultimately be yours. You may be able to manage your child's behaviour better if there is no one else there for them to plead with or seek solace from. However it is important to remember that everyone needs a little time out occasionally and, as a single parent, you may feel this is much harder to achieve.

You may also worry about the lack of a male or female role model in your child's life. Of course, many of these problems can, and have, been successfully overcome with the help of a good support network of friends and family. If friends or family members offer to take your child off your hands for a couple of hours don't be a martyr and refuse their help – they will stop offering if you don't take them up. Instead, pack your child off, put your feet up and enjoy a couple of hours of child-free relaxation!

## …cing
## …viour

…xts, however it is not the
…e, it is the way in which
…f concern. Providing the
…and appropriate manner,
…mptions to be made.

## The nuclear family

This kind of family is often referred to as the 'average' family. The nuclear family consists of both parents living with their biological children.

## The extended family

This kind of family was traditional in the UK for many years and is still very common in many parts of the world today. Extended families consist of parents and children living together in a close-knit community with grandparents, aunts, uncles and cousins. Extended families vary enormously, but often much of the childcare is left up to family members and, in some cases, grandmothers are considered the most important people in the family and most of the child rearing is their responsibility.

Living within such a close-knit community usually means that family members are on hand to help out with the family and offer support. However, it can often be difficult for parents of the children, particularly women, to reach their full potential because of the constant input from other family members. The hierarchy involved can strip parents of status or authority.

## The gay and lesbian family

These types of families are made up of either the children living with one natural parent along with the parent's partner of the same sex or when the children have been adopted by a couple of the same sex. There is little evidence as yet about the effects on children growing up with gay or lesbian parents as this type of family structure is relatively new.

## The single or one-parent family

This type of family structure consists of one parent living on their own with the children. Single or one-parent families may be as a result of the parents having gone through a divorce or separation, when one parent has died or through personal choice, for example, when the mother has decided to have a baby without wanting the support of the father. One of the problems which single or one-parent families may face is the financial and emotional implications of providing for a child with no support from a partner.

## The reconstituted family

This is where the children live with one natural parent and one step-parent. In some cases the children of the step-parent may also live in the house. The main potential problem with this type of family structure is that there may be confusion with regard to authority. For example, a child living with their natural mother and her new husband, the child's step-father, may resent someone taking their biological father's place and find it hard to take instructions from their step-father. Likewise, jealousy and resentment experienced by the natural father, who is not able to live with his child, may also be experienced.

Another potential issue with this kind of family set-up is in the form of 'weekend parents'. When parents only see their children at the weekend or, in some cases, every other weekend, they may be tempted to spoil them to make up for the time they have lost. This can lead to problems with discipline when the children return to their regular family set-up and confusion about boundaries and rules may set in.

## The adoptive family

This type of family consists of two parents living with a child who is not biologically their own. In some cases the child may not be aware that they have been adopted and this type of family would then take on the role of a nuclear or extended family set-up.

## The foster family

These families consist of children being placed with foster parents for varying lengths of time. Very often children are placed with foster parents if they are going through child protection issues.

## The mixed ethnic family

This type of family set-up consists of children living with parents of differing religions, beliefs or cultures from the other. Problems may arise if the children become confused as to which religion or culture they belong to.

## The nomadic family

This type of family is usually associated with gypsies or travellers. Children are surrounded by other family members and close friends. Nomadic families have no permanent town or village and spend their time moving around. The main problem for children living within this type of family set-up is the limited opportunity for them to put down roots and make friends. Their education may also suffer due to lack of regular schooling.

# Diet

Research has shown that some children show unacceptable patterns of behaviour, such as hyperactivity, sleeping problems and temper tantrums which could be as a result of the additives within their diet. As a result of this research many supermarkets are now producing foods which are additive-free.

## Additives

Additives are added to packaged food for several reasons:

- to preserve its shelf life
- to make it look better
- to make it taste better.

All manufactured food must, by law, display labels identifying the ingredients present in the food and listing them in order, starting with the largest amount present. Additives are identified on packaging by an 'E number'. An E number is the code number which is recognised within the European Community.

Additives are usually grouped as follows:

| | |
|---|---|
| **Antioxidants** | These are natural substances such as lecithin (E322) and chemicals such as butylated hydroxyanisole (E320). |
| **Artificial sweeteners** | These are substances such as saccharin and sorbitol (E420). |
| **Colourings** | These are substances such as tartrazine (E102), sunset yellow (E110) and caramels (E150). |
| **Emulsifiers and stabilisers** | These are substances such as gum arabic (E414) and locust bean gum (E410). |
| **Flavourings** | These are substances which include all herbs and spices along with monosodium glutamate (621 MSG). |

**Preservatives** These are substances such as sorbic acid (E200) and sulphur dioxide (E220).

Although additives can have a negative impact on the health of children and cause behaviour problems each of the above additives has a purpose.

- **Antioxidants** prevent fatty foods from becoming stale and help to protect the vitamins in the food from being destroyed during processing.
- **Artificial sweeteners** are useful for low-calorie foods and are also used in specially-prepared foods such as those designed for diabetics.
- **Colourings** are used to make food look more colourful and attractive.
- **Emulsifiers** are used when mixing together foodstuffs which would normally separate. The use of emulsifiers ensures that the food maintains the mixed quality so that separation does not occur after the food has been processed.
- **Flavourings** are used to enhance or increase the flavour or the food.
- **Preservatives** are used to increase the length of the food's shelf life and to prevent the food becoming spoilt by microbes.

## Overseeing the quality of your child's diet

It is important, when choosing foods, that you carefully check the content for additives and choose foods which do not contain an excessive amount of unnecessary E numbers.

If you have a child who is prone to temper tantrums, hyperactivity or behaviour-related problems you will need to be extra vigilant as studies have shown an intolerance to tartrazine may trigger these problems. Unfortunately tartrazine can be found in many foodstuffs specifically aimed at children, such as sweets and soft drinks.

## Providing a healthy balanced diet

A healthy balanced diet is something that we would all benefit from, however it is important to remember that childhood eating patterns and habits determine adult food tastes in later life.

### *Nutrients*

In order for the body to grow and develop it requires nutrients. There are five types of nutrients and these are:

*Proteins*

Proteins help the body to grow and assist the healing process. Proteins can be found in:

- meat
- fish
- soya
- vegetables
- dairy products such as milk, cheese, yoghurt.

*Vitamins*

Vitamins are essential to growth and development. Vitamins can be found in:

- fruit
- vegetables
- most fresh foods.

*Fats*

Fats provide the body with energy, however they are only required in moderate amounts in order to maintain a healthy balanced diet. Fats can be found in:

- meat
- fish

- vegetable oils
- dairy products such as milk, cheese, yoghurt.

*Minerals*

Minerals, such as calcium, are required for healthy teeth and strong bones. Iron is needed to boost energy levels and prevent anaemia. Minerals can be found in:

- dairy products (calcium)
- red meat (iron)
- some green vegetables (iron).

*Carbohydrates*

Carbohydrates provide the body with energy. Carbohydrates can be found in:

- potatoes
- bread
- bananas
- vegetables.

## Checking food labels

It is likely that you will have your own opinions as to issues such as chemical additives and genetically-modified products, however you should get into the habit of checking food labels when you shop and take into account the nutritional value of the food you buy. Look closely at the amount of salt and sugar that has been added.

## Avoiding processed and prepared foods

Unfortunately, in the times that we live in, most children eat too many fast-food products, processed foods, fizzy drinks, sweets, chocolate, biscuits, crisps and so on, all of which are the main food groups which contain the very additives that are often associated with unacceptable behaviour, poor concentration and hyperactivity in children. The increase in the consumption of these foods is leading to long-term health problems throughout the world and the lack of consumption of foods which are good for us, such as fruit, meat, fish, vegetables and dairy products, is resulting in a poor diet.

The reason why processed and prepared foods are so appealing is quite simply because they save us time. Although I am not suggesting that you start baking your own bread and cakes, I am suggesting that you begin to look at how you can provide your children with an adequate intake of fresh foods and hold back on the processed foods which are causing our children to become increasingly unhealthy.

Although there has been concern about the possible links between children's behaviour and preservatives and food colouring for many years, it is perhaps due to the dismissive attitudes of the government and food manufacturers that no action has been taken. However, we are now witnessing reports of obesity in children as young as three years old and it is becoming widely acknowledged that a poor diet and lack of exercise is having a detrimental affect on the health of our children.

Allowing children to snack on crisps and sweets because it is convenient and quick is not an acceptable excuse for parents to be putting their children's health at risk. We need to look carefully at the amount of salt and sugar our children are consuming on a daily basis and compare these to the recommended daily intake – it makes for a startling discovery in some cases.

## Education, not re-education

Children, if trained correctly from the onset, will be just as happy to snack on fresh fruit, carrot sticks or dried fruit and substitute fizzy drinks for water. Many parents will scoff at this idea but their children only prefer the foodstuffs which are bad for them because this is what they have been given and what they have grown to expect. Teaching children about eating a healthy diet from the beginning is much easier than re-educating them at a later date when the harm to their bodies has begun and they may already be craving a high sugar or salt intake.

Use your imagination to create interesting meals and snacks which look appealing but which are full of healthy, nutritional ingredients. Occasional treats are acceptable and there is no need to blitz the house of all traces of unhealthy food. It is when fresh foods and balanced meals are being substituted for unhealthy snacks that the problems really begin to set in. In time you will get into the habit of shopping healthily and, let's face it, if you don't buy the offending foods your children won't be tempted to eat them.

### Tips

Start by limiting the amount of biscuits and crisps you buy during your weekly shop and increasing the amount of fresh fruit and vegetables. To save time cooking and preparing meals try to make batches of healthy foods to store in the freezer. If you do this at a weekend when you are not out at work then you will be able to provide your family with a healthy, balanced meal every day of the week without spending hours preparing it at the end of a busy working day. There is more on diet and nutrition in Part Two.

## Divorce and separation

Over a quarter of all babies born in the UK today are likely to experience parental separation before they reach school leaving age. Although no one can really be sure how divorce or separation of a child's parents will affect them until later on in their lives, it has to be acknowledged that marital break-ups are one of the most common adverse life events experienced by children.

It is not unusual for children to experience a whole range of feelings and emotions including:

- sadness
- anger

- grief
- guilt
- lack of confidence
- mistrust
- fear
- rejection.

## Ensuring your child's stability

It is very important that parents acknowledge their children's feelings and allow them to talk openly about the marriage or partnership break-up if they are old enough to do so. Children need routine and structure in their lives and divorce and separation will have a huge impact on this. It is necessary for *both* parents to work together to reassure the children that they are still very much loved and cared for, however acrimonious the break up may be.

Children need to have their feelings and welfare taken into account and it has to be understood that, no matter how amicable a divorce or separation is and no matter how often the parents will deny it, it *will* have an impact on the children involved. Just how drastic an impact it has will be, in the long run, down to the parents.

In an ideal world, even after a divorce or separation, both parents would see the children on a regular basis and have equal input in their lives. However we do not live in an ideal world and in some cases this is simply not possible. Some children will have to cut all ties with a parent following a divorce or separation, they may move to another area or even another country and lose contact with family and friends, all of which will add to the distress they are already experiencing.

It is important that neither parent apportions blame to the other in front of the child and that both parents are on hand to help and support the child through this difficult period. Try to stick to usual routines as much as possible. Remember, although divorce and separation are often unpleasant they are not insurmountable and life will return to normality once everyone has a chance to come to term with events. The trick is not to hide what is happening or shut the child out if they obviously wish to talk to you about the situation. Answer their questions and concerns as honestly and as openly as you can within their boundaries of age and understanding.

## Common reactions to parents' divorce

The majority of children's reactions to divorce can be summarised in the following ways:

- **Pre-school children** are unlikely to understand the full implications of divorce. They may appear sad and frightened when their parents separate. It is common for pre-school children to become clingy and exhibit demanding behaviour. They may show aggression and have problems sleeping.
- **Primary school-aged children** are likely to experience sadness and grief when their parents separate. However most will also display anger, particularly towards the parent with whom they are living. Blame is usually apportioned to the remaining parent whilst the absent one tends to be idolised.
- **Pre-adolescent children** are likely to understand the full implications of their parents' separation however, because they experience pain and embarrassment acutely, they may be unwilling or unable to talk about their feelings leading to fears and concerns being bottled up. They may appear unconcerned and seek solace in other distractions. Often children of this age will side with one parent and may even refuse to see the other.
- **Adolescents** are likely to experience a range of emotions and may even withdraw from family life. It is during this time that some children may go off the rails seeking solace, for example, in friends who may be unsuitable and have a detrimental affect on their wellbeing.

Whilst some children will cope admirably, shrug off the past and get on with making new friends and may even look at the whole episode as an adventure, others will not be so resilient and may take a long time to adjust to their new circumstances. They may become quiet and withdrawn, fearing future rejection if they build up a new network of friends, or they may become attention seeking and difficult to handle.

## Death

Death, like divorce and separation, can affect a child very deeply. However, it is important to remember that some children will find the finality of death a difficult concept to grasp and may well resort to asking for the dead person for some time afterwards.

A child's perception of death can be very confused and very deep; at times they may seem to trivialise it by likening death to other losses such as mislaying a favourite toy. The upset and dismay felt by both will trigger feelings of confusion and bewilderment and often parents fall into the trap of thinking that a child has not really been affected by the death if they can liken it to losing a favourite teddy bear, for example. But considering that the child's favourite teddy bear may be an object of great comfort and joy to the child and something that they usually have with them 24 hours a day, taking this away will indeed cause great distress.

A child may grieve for a long time and then, when you think that they have finally come to terms with the situation, they may revert back and begin asking for the deceased person again. You will need to show lots of patience and sensitivity and answer any questions and concerns they may have as openly and honestly as possible. The child may become clingy and moody and be prone to temper tantrums whilst going through this traumatic period.

## Siblings

If you have more than one child you don't need me to tell you all about sibling rivalry. The way you deal with your children collectively will determine the kind of relationship they have with one another many years down the line. If you separate them and treat them differently you will divide them, if you treat them as equals they will bond together and hopefully remain close friends for life.

The saying 'blood is thicker than water' does not apply to all families and unfortunately some siblings grow away from one another as they grow older. Comparing children to one another is a sure sign of developing jealousy and rivalry and this should be avoided at all costs. Remember they may be all your children but they are also individuals and therefore should be treated as such. No-one likes to be compared to someone else, particularly if this is less favourably.

Siblings will argue and fight, of that there is no doubt – this is perfectly natural behaviour for children living and growing up together. However, no child should feel inferior or second best to their older or, in some cases, younger siblings.

## Allowing disagreements between siblings

Allowing children to squabble, within reason, actually does help them believe it or not. It teaches them the importance of compromise and helps them to learn how to deal with conflict and adversity. Sibling fall-outs are all about power struggles when the children learn how to achieve independence, amongst other important life skills.

## Accepting a new baby into the family

Accepting a new baby into the family can be very difficult for any child, but if the child has been used to having their parents' undivided attention for several years before the baby comes along this can really put a spanner in the works. Feelings of jealousy and insecurity may well surface.

A large number of new mothers experience the 'baby blues' after the birth when they feel tired, anxious and stressed. Although this may only last for a few days, it can be a frightening time. The work involved in looking after a new baby, coupled with the lack of sleep, often makes it difficult for new parents to spend quality time with their older children. It is absolutely vital that this is not overlooked as it is quite possible that your older child or children will be feeling anxious and left out. Often all that is needed to keep their feelings of insecurity at bay is your reassurance.

# Illness

Illness can have a massive impact on a child's behaviour and it is often the two or three days before a diagnosis has been made when the child is coming down with something when their behaviour gives cause for concern. Once the symptoms are evident it is much easier to make excuses for their behaviour. Often before the symptoms appear the child can feel tired and irritable and this can have a huge impact on the way they behave.

Parents need to make certain allowances for illness but should not let their children get away with things they wouldn't normally be allowed to as this will only lead to confusion and problems when the child is back to full health.

## Dealing with serious illness

Long-term illnesses may prove very difficult, particularly if the child has a very severe or life-threatening condition. Many parents feel guilty at the suffering their child is going through and as such they tend to over-compensate and allow them free rein. Even in very severe cases, this is seldom a good idea. Children need boundaries in order for them to feel loved, valued and secure and, if anything, when a child is suffering through illness this is when they crave the kind of reassurance that boundaries provide all the more.

# Culture

Diversity is all about differences and we need to accept and embrace the many differences there are in people whether these be physical differences, social differences, emotional differences, sexual differences or cultural differences. It is the way in which we are perceived by other people which will ultimately mould our behaviour towards others. For example, if a child experiences racism due to a difference in their cultural upbringing and beliefs they are more likely to respond to this racism either by withdrawing from the situation or becoming aggressive, neither of which is a healthy option to adopt. Everyone has the right to equal respect, opportunity and justice and it is important that we, as parents, teach these important values to our children so that they in turn can learn about the importance of diversity and equality.

## Moving house or school

To some children moving house or school and ultimately losing friends can be likened to bereavement. The child will experience the same sense of loss and abandonment and may struggle to come to terms with not seeing their old friends as frequently as they have done in the past.

Children place a lot of emphasis on the security of familiar surroundings and people and, instead of seeing the whole episode as an adventure, as you would probably like to expect, they may become anxious and withdrawn. Even from a very young age children are capable of forging worthwhile and meaningful friendships and it can be a huge wrench to a child to have these friendships brought to an abrupt end. They may find it difficult to make new friends quickly at their new school or in their new neighbourhood and this may exacerbate their feelings of loss.

Try to be patient in these circumstances and give your child plenty of warnings about the move so that they can be prepared well in advance. If possible allow them to keep in touch with their old friends, although care should be taken in case hanging on to past friends hinders the making of new ones.

## Unemployment

Although unemployment may not appear to be something that would immediately affect the way in which a child behaves and, in some cases, it could be argued that because parents do not go out to work they can spend more time playing with their child and is therefore beneficial to the child, there will come a time, perhaps when the child is a little older and experiences peer pressure, when their unemployed parents will cause resentment. The child may be embarrassed by the lack of money their parents have to spend on them and resent not being able to have the luxuries of expensive toys, clothes and holidays that perhaps their friends' parents can afford to lavish on them. This will inevitably affect the way in which the child behaves.

## Disability

Like illness, disability is one of the factors which parents tend to use as an excuse for a child's unacceptable behaviour. Although it is important to appreciate and be aware of how the child's behaviour may be affected if they are unwell or have a serious disability, neither should be used as an excuse to allow the child to behave in an unreasonable manner.

Children suffering from a severe disability may, at times, consider themselves to be a burden to their family and friends and feel unsure of themselves and their own abilities. They may resort to testing how much their parents love them by exhibiting unreasonable behaviour or making excessive demands. They may even resort to apportioning blame to those they consider responsible for their disability. Children in these circumstances need endless love, reassurance and praise however, like able-bodied children, they also need boundaries in order to feel secure and safe.

## Gender

Our own opinions and ideas will influence the way in which we respond to stereotypical views of gender-based activities and how we would feel if the roles were reversed. Some parents would be horrified to catch their son pushing a doll's pram around but is this really something to be frowned upon? How many fathers do just that with their own babies? Boys, just like girls, need to be able to explore their gentle, nurturing side and should not be encouraged to take part in only masculine activities. If you want your son to express his own feelings and take into account the feelings of others then he needs to know how to be sensitive and learn to care for others. Parents, it seems, tend to accept boyish behaviour in girls more readily than feminine behaviour in boys.

# Why do I need to manage my child's behaviour?

## Why does my child misbehave?

Before we go any further with this question let me firstly reassure you that all children misbehave from time to time. Children are not born pre-programmed with an innate ability to behave well and do exactly as they are told. They need to test the waters so to speak, and discover for themselves what they will be allowed to do. Children are inquisitive by nature and will explore their environment, seeking entertainment and fun.

## Thinking about unacceptable behaviour

Take some time to think about how children learn what is and is not acceptable. Cast your mind back to things your own children are allowed to do. Have they ever been tempted to draw on the walls for example? If so, how did you respond? How is your 14-month old child supposed to know that they are not allowed to draw on the walls with your expensive lipstick unless you make it perfectly clear to them that they aren't supposed to? Is this kind of behaviour really naughty? Of course if you applied the same question to an eight year old who had just done the same thing your answer would, most likely, be very different. What you need to ask yourself here is why will an eight year old know that this behaviour is unacceptable when the 14-month old thinks it is fun? The answer of course is because you have taught your eight year old right from wrong and she knows that this is not behaviour which is acceptable to you, whereas your 14-month old is still learning.

## Reasons for misbehaving

Children misbehave for a variety of reasons; lack of understanding is just one of these reasons. They may also act in an unacceptable manner because:

- They are bored
- They are tired
- They are unwell
- They are frightened
- They are anxious
- They are frustrated
- They feel restricted
- They are seeking attention
- They are copying what they think others are doing
- They are unaware of any potential damage they are causing or danger they may be in
- They are unable to control their emotions or feelings
- They are feeling left out or treated unfairly
- They are feeling unsettled or confused
- They do not have clear, consistent boundaries to follow
- They have a particular learning difficulty.

Let us look at the reasons why a child may misbehave in more detail and how we can successfully manage each factor.

### Boredom

Children often resort to unwanted behaviour when they are bored. Providing adequate toys or activities which stimulate, excite and capture a child's imagination and creativity can be an excellent outlet for boredom and will dissuade children from looking for unacceptable ways of entertaining themselves. However, it is still important to make time for your child, to play with them, talk to them and, most importantly, to listen to them. Of course, toys are important learning tools for children, but adults are by far the most important 'toy' a child can have.

If your child appears to break the toys you buy them, do not immediately condemn them and accuse them of intentionally spoiling things. Ask yourself if the child knows *how* to play with the toy. Have you taken the time to show them what the toy does and how is should be played with or did you give them the box and expect them to 'get on with it' whilst you busied yourself with other tasks at hand?

When choosing toys or activities for your child, always take their age and development into account. We all like to think our children are mini Einsteins, but setting a task which is too complex or selecting a toy which is aimed at a child several years older than your own will not encourage them to be clever. On the contrary, being unrealistic with your expectations of your child's ability will result in frustration and may even set your child's progress back as they struggle to try to achieve the impossible targets you have set.

## Tiredness

Allowing a child to stay up very late or not giving them the opportunity to rest or sleep when they need to during the day will inevitably result in a tired, restless and irritable child whose exhaustion will be shown in unacceptable behaviour. The simple solution to this is to set appropriate bedtimes and stick to them. If your child has had a broken night's sleep due to illness, let them have a nap during the day to refresh themselves if necessary.

## Illness

Unlike feeling tired, if your child is unwell there is little you can do except look after them and wait for them to regain complete health once again. Illness is usually short lived and your child will return to their old self in a few days' time.

## Feeling frightened or anxious

In much the same way as adults' behaviour will vary depending on how they deal with these emotions so too will your child's. Children who are experiencing bullying at school, for example, may be frightened or anxious and, as a result, they may resort to destructive behaviour as a way of venting their frustration and resentment because of what they are experiencing. It is important that you talk to your child and find out what is upsetting them in order for you to help them work through their problems.

## Frustration

Young children can experience frustration for many reasons. They may still be learning how to communicate and their lack of communication skills can lead to frustration which is often shown in temper tantrums. Your child may well know exactly what he wants but his inability to let you know in a way that you can understand will lead to frustration. Children who are not yet mobile may also feel frustrated if they are unable to crawl or walk and toys are not within their reach.

## Being restricted

Being restricted through lack of mobility can lead to inappropriate behaviour. A child who has been sitting in a highchair or placed in a play pen for too long may become agitated at the restrictions placed on them. Likewise, parents who are over cautious with their children because they fear they may come to some harm will make them frustrated with the restrictions they place on them. This too can result in unacceptable behaviour. It is important that parents acknowledge their children's abilities and allow them the appropriate freedom they need in order to grow and mature.

## Attention seeking

We often hear adults saying, 'Take no notice of him, he's just attention seeking,' but what exactly do we mean by this? Surely if a child is showing unacceptable behaviour and their parent sees this as 'attention seeking' the answer would be to put a stop to it by giving the child your attention? Some children are by nature overly seeking of attention. In certain situations this can prove a problem. An example is in the classroom if the teacher has 30 pupils to teach. The child who needs to be seen as the 'only child' will end up feeling ignored when in fact they are simply expected to take their turn and are being treated in the same way as the other 29 pupils.

Attention-seeking behaviour may be a result of being brought up by parents whose lives have revolved around their child and also see no reason why their child should not receive their undivided attention. The problems start here when the child has difficulty understanding that this cannot happen in every situation. On the other hand, children who constantly appear to seek attention may do so because they are actually being deprived of the attention they need. They will therefore resort to unacceptable behaviour in order to gain it.

## Copying others

Can we really say that a three year old is being naughty because they have pulled up all the flowers in the garden after watching you weed the flower bed? How can they really be expected to know the difference between a daffodil and a dandelion? Likewise if they see you rant and rave, throw things and fly off the handle when things go wrong, would it be such a surprise to witness them doing the same when they can't have their own way? Children learn many things through imitation and behaviour is one of those things.

## Unaware of what they are doing

Sometimes children can appear to be behaving inappropriately, however it could be that they are unaware of any damage they are causing or any danger they may be putting themselves or others in. This could be down to the fact that they are either too young to understand the consequences of their actions or they have never been taught about this type of danger. You can avoid this kind of inappropriate behaviour by teaching children about danger and the importance of keeping safe and respecting other people and their property.

## Unable to control emotions or feelings

Young children often find it difficult to control their emotions or feelings and resort to lashing out or temper tantrums when things are not going their way. Frustration is, once again, a sign of this pent-up anger and the ability to curb one's temper and act in a reasonable and responsible manner comes with age and experience. Always try to present your child with a positive role model by remaining calm and refraining from shouting or becoming angry when dealing with inappropriate behaviour.

## Feeling left out or treated unfairly

If you have ever felt that you are being treated unfairly or overlooked you may well understand the reasons why a child may exhibit unacceptable behaviour if they are experiencing similar feelings. The child may become resentful and their pride will be hurt. Being made to think that they are inconsequential or second best can have a profound affect on a young child and they may resort to tantrums in a bid to seek 'justice' for themselves and gain the recognition they feel they deserve. Sometimes well-behaved children might feel left out as they often tend to get overlooked.

## Feeling unsettled or confused

Feelings of confusion can be quite frightening to a child. Young children need the security of a routine and sometimes even the slightest of changes can upset them. If possible try to stick to familiar routines and if changes are necessary make sure you give your child plenty of warning and prepare them for what to expect.

### Not having clear or consistent boundaries to follow

Children need to learn right from wrong and they can only do this successfully in a loving environment with rules which are easy to understand and which are consistent. Parents who continually alter these rules or give in to persuasion are likely to create confused children who are unsure of how to act. Set your rules and stick to them. Although flexibility may sometimes be needed, try to avoid changing your decisions too much or allowing your child to win you over just to keep the peace.

### Learning difficulties

Although learning difficulties can not strictly be classed as misbehaviour it is important that parents do not over-compensate for their child if they do have a learning difficulty. Often children even with very severe learning problems are capable of displaying acceptable behaviour most of the time and this should be encouraged whenever possible rather than excuses made when the child is acting inappropriately.

## How children learn about behaviour

One thing we can be sure of is that there is always a reason for the way in which a child, or for that matter an adult, behaves. Something, however inconsequential or trivial it may seem, affects the way in which we behave. Whether we are happy, sad, elated, excited, apprehensive, fearful or indifferent, our feelings will have an affect on our behaviour and our willingness or, in some cases, unwillingness to cooperate.

Before we can begin to change the way in which our children behave we must first come to understand *why* they are acting in a certain way in the first place and where they have learned this type of behaviour.

Babies are not born knowing how to behave well or how to misbehave. They have no idea at all about what is socially acceptable and do not know how to behave in any particular way. You may have heard a mother complain because her baby cries all night and sleeps all day, but it is important to understand that the child's behaviour is not intentional. As a baby, he is incapable of thinking or behaving in an 'unacceptable' manner. The baby has not decided in advance to keep his mother awake all night, rather he is acting instinctively. He may be uncomfortable, be suffering from colic or simply want to be cuddled when he cries all night – what he most definitely is not being is naughty.

## Ways of learning behaviour

There are, of course, many different reasons for a child's behaviour and, as each child is unique, it is impossible to list every possible trait or attribute that causes each child to behave in a certain way. However, there are three main ways in which children actually learn *how* to behave and these are from:

- parents or carers
- other people
- influences inside and outside the home.

### *Parents and carers*

Children often emulate their parents; they look up to them and strive to be like them. It is for this reason that we must be vigilant and display good behaviour at all times. Our children will pick up on the way we behave and teaching them correctly from the outset is far easier than undoing bad behaviour and re-educating children further down the line.

The way in which we respond to our children when their behaviour falls short of our expectations is also very important, as this will have a lasting impact on them. How you relate to your child will in turn teach them how to relate to others and it is vital that this is taught successfully.

### *Other people*

As our children get older and begin to mix with others, perhaps at nursery or school, they will gradually begin to spend less and less time with their parents and carers and will become more open to outside influences. Children will learn to mix with other children and will gradually become more and more aware of how other people behave and respond to certain situations. Peer pressure and authoritative role models, such as teachers, can have a strong influence on the way in which our children behave. In some cases the desire to please these other people can impact negatively on what the child has been taught at home as they begin to question your parental authority and perhaps even rebel against the rules they have been expected to follow in the past.

### *Influences inside and outside the home*

These kinds of influences can include television, newspapers, video games and so on, all of which can portray both positive and negative images about behaviour. Although it is relatively easy to protect our children from negative influences inside the home, providing we take an interest in what they are doing and regulate their television viewing, video games and internet access, it can be much harder to keep track of the influences they are being introduced to outside the home.

## Adapting your parenting approach to each child

Many parents feel that managing their children's behaviour should come naturally and that because they know their own children better than anyone else they think getting them to behave should be relatively easy. Nothing could be further from the truth. Children from the same family, even identical twins, can be very different in personality and although you may think that you have brought all of your children up in the same manner with the same rules and boundaries do not be fooled into thinking that this means that they will all turn out the same!

Sometimes keeping our own emotions and behaviour in check can be difficult and being responsible for ensuring that another person behaves well can be very daunting. To reiterate, all children will misbehave some of the time and this is perfectly normal – it is all part of growing up, testing the boundaries and learning how to become socially acceptable.

# Behaviour inside the home

## Keeping one set of rules

Many parents fall into the trap of having two sets of rules when it comes to managing their children's behaviour. The first set of rules are to be used inside the home and the second set outside the home. The message given to the child in these circumstances is that behaviour can be modified depending on where you are.

Whilst it may be easy to turn a blind eye when your child is misbehaving at home you should always stop and think how you would feel if they were exhibiting this kind of behaviour in public. If it causes you concern then it is paramount that you put a stop to it. Like it or not, your child will probably think that what they are doing is acceptable and they will repeat it, probably in public next time.

## Amusing but inappropriate behaviour

Another trap which many parents of young children in particular seem to fall into is laughing at their toddler's 'inappropriate' behaviour. I don't doubt for one minute that there have been many times when you have watched your child do or say something inappropriate, but the sheer innocence of their actions has brought you to your knees in hysterics – I know because I too have been guilty of this. However, despite seeing the funny side of things, and children can be very amusing at times, it is important not to give out mixed messages.

My own children have been guilty of saying things which, to an outsider, would appear rude and even though admittedly at times I agreed with what they said and wished I too had the nerve to air my opinions, I did stifle my laugh and reprimand them. Next to pushing boundaries, children also love to amuse and if they are aware that you thought their behaviour was funny they will look for other ways to amuse you.

## Being consistent

Set your rules and make sure you play by them at every opportunity. Your child may well have difficulty playing by one set of rules and will probably play up enough as it is, so by introducing rules for at home and rules for in public you are simply asking for trouble. Children need to learn all about respect and social acceptance and this should come naturally to them in time if they have been taught well from the beginning.

## Showing respect

Respect can not be commanded: it must be earned. Just as your child needs to earn your respect so too will you need to earn respect from your child. Being a parent does not give you an automatic right to be shown courtesy and respect. If you treat your child with no respect and simply expect them to do as they are told without giving them reasonable boundaries to follow, you will be heading for disaster. It is important therefore that parents see respect as a two-way situation.

Teachers complain that the children in their classes show them no respect, police officers complain that teenagers are unruly and have no respect and the older generation are often heard saying that children showed respect back in the 'good old days'. So what exactly is respect? What does the word conjure up for you personally? Are you a respectful person? Do you find it easy to respect people and their property? Do you feel you command respect in return?

## Defining respect

The dictionary's definition of respect is 'consideration for the feelings or rights of others'. Respect means being polite, kind and caring. It means showing thoughtfulness and consideration. It means being helpful, civil and courteous. Showing respect and earning respect are probably two of the most difficult aspects we have to learn, and with so many disrespectful adults in society today is it really such a huge surprise to find that children sometimes struggle with this important task?

## Respecting your children

As I have previously said, to gain respect we must firstly give respect. So in what ways can parents respect their children? The simple answer to this question is to treat your children in a manner that you personally would like to be treated by them. Talk to your child in a respectful manner and explain what you expect from them without resorting to humiliation or accusations.

## Remaining calm

Showing respect begins by remaining calm. Reveal to your children how difficult situations can be resolved amicably without resorting to shouting and violence. Express love and kindness towards your children. Set realistic boundaries and keep your expectations of their behaviour fair but firm.

## Taking your children's feelings into account

It is very important that children have their feelings taken into consideration. They need to feel loved and valued and, above all else, they need you to listen to them and respond to them. Listening to your child and valuing their opinions and wishes does not mean having to please them all of the time, nor does it mean that by voicing their wishes they must have them met. It simply means that their opinions are taken into account and, if you are unable to meet them, you can at least show that you have considered them. This will go a long way to showing your child that you respect and value their views.

## How to show your children respect

In order to show your children respect you need to:

- Listen to what they have to say
- Take their opinions and wishes into account
- Avoid embarrassing them in public
- Show them love and kindness
- Use appropriate discipline with a fair but firm approach.

You may often feel like the villain when it comes to disciplining your child, however rest assured the parents who set realistic boundaries and expect their children to behave well most of the time will be the parents whose children respect them.

Children will respond better to fewer rules quite simply because they will find it easier to remember. If you set rules, but then give in to pressure when your child moans or resists, then you will lose any form of authority as a parent and the respect your children have for you will diminish. Contrary to what children actually say, they *do* need boundaries set by loving parents, whose aim is to protect and nurture their children. They need the security of a loving home where they can feel safe to explore and try out new and exciting things and they can only do this if they feel confident and valued.

## Gaining respect from your children

In order to gain respect from your children you need to:

- Set your rules and stick to them
- Set only rules which are necessary – the fewer the better
- Have clear and consistent boundaries

- Be firm but fair
- When you say no you must mean no and avoid giving in to tantrums or persuasion.

## Setting boundaries

Routines are essential to the wellbeing of toddlers and young children. Young children learn by repetition, they like to hear the same story being read over and over again and enjoy singing the same songs and nursery rhymes. This is because they can get a sense of control over the situation if they have some idea of what to expect.

### Setting a routine

Ideally parents will set a routine for their children every day which will include waking up, having breakfast, getting dressed, playing, shopping, lunchtime, nap, outing, teatime, bathtime and bedtime. Obviously how flexible your routine is will depend very much on your own daily commitments and, if you are a working parent, your child will probably be spending some of their time in day care or at school. Nurseries, schools and childminders will also have routines and your child will soon begin to understand what is going to happen and be able to anticipate things. A major change in their routine such as starting a new school or nursery setting can have a huge impact on a child's behaviour because their routine is being threatened and they have no control over what to expect.

### Building a safety zone

When setting boundaries you are effectively building a 'safety zone' around your child. Remain in the zone and the child learns how to cooperate and play in safety and in an acceptable manner, stray outside the zone and it may be necessary to reprimand them.

If you fail to deal with your child's behaviour in a consistent way it will lead to further difficulties down the line. Your child needs to know the rules you have set in order for them to feel safe and they need to understand why these rules are in place. However it is also important, if your child spends some of their time in day care or at school, that they understand that the boundaries in these settings may differ from those you have at home. They will need to adopt the rules of the new setting when they are there. Again this can at times be confusing for a child, particularly if they are very young, and it may be necessary for you to work with your child's nursery nurse or childminder in order to ensure consistency between the day care setting and home.

For example, a child who spends some time with a childminder may find themselves being restricted to certain parts of the house. If your child is used to wandering through their own house as and when they feel like it they may find it difficult to understand why they are not allowed in the bedrooms at the childminder's house. Explaining any differences in rules and boundaries will appear reasonable and consistent if they seem simple and fair to the child.

## Writing down your expectations

Unlike day-care establishments most homes will not have written rules and expectations when it comes to managing children's behaviour. It may, however, be a good idea for you to jot down the expectations you have of your children's behaviour so that you can look at them clearly. If you make a list of the framework you have set for dealing with your children's behaviour you will be able to see easily whether this framework will be effective. Ask yourself a few simple questions and answer them honestly. By doing this, you should be able to see whether the boundaries you have set are realistic, useful and workable:

- Are your rules easy for you to understand?
- Are your rules easy for your child to understand?
- Are all your rules necessary?
- Are all your rules fair?

- Are your rules positive?
- Is your child able to stick to the rules most of the time?

If you have answered 'no' to any of these questions it might be a good idea to start again and review your rules.

# Behaviour outside the home

## Social acceptance

Children should be able to relax and be themselves in the security of their own home. However it is essential, if they are showing unacceptable behaviour, that they are reprimanded regardless of whether they are at home or not.

We all have to learn that some behaviour is simply not considered acceptable in public. For example we know, as adults, that we can not walk into a shop and take something just because we want it. Young children, on the other hand, are still learning and it comes as no surprise if a toddler has helped themselves from the sweet display placed near the checkout in a supermarket whilst their mother is paying for the shopping. How are they supposed to know that they have to pay for the sweets? Of course, the child is not intentionally shop lifting, however their behaviour needs to be kept in check if you are to avoid a repeat performance, perhaps when the child is older and expected to know better.

Social acceptance comes in many forms. Children need to learn how to act in public, eat in public and make and maintain friendships; all of these skills need to be mastered successfully if they are to become socially accepted.

## Maintaining self-respect

At the heart of children's social relationships is their ability to maintain self-respect, whilst at the same time extending respect to others. It is by demonstrating respect through our actions which really makes a difference in society. We can help children to put respect into action by teaching them manners, but the manners must be sincere and well intentioned if they are to be authentic rather than superficial.

We can only become credible role models for our children if we practise what we preach so, next time you are about to moan at the length of the queue or because the driver in front of you has failed to use their indicators, think about how your actions may affect your child's understanding of how best to conduct their own behaviour.

## Starting young

Although the majority of social acceptance develops as the child matures and begins to understand exactly what is expected of them, it is important that parents plant the seeds of positive social acceptance from a very young age. It is paramount that you don't give in to your child if they are having a tantrum for example.

If your child is throwing a tantrum in the supermarket because they can't have something, giving in because they are creating a scene is telling them that tantrums get them what they want. Rest assured, they will repeat the performance at every opportunity if they think their behaviour will be rewarded. Instead, try ignoring the behaviour. If this is impossible and, let's face it, children's temper tantrums can resemble mini hurricanes, then leave your shopping, pick up your child and take them home. There may not be any food in the cupboards for tea but at least you will have escaped the horrendous scene in the supermarket when every other shopper appears to be condemning you for being the worst mother on earth.

Your child will learn, relatively quickly, that tantrums are a waste of time providing you do not reward them when they resort to one.

# Behaving appropriately in public

Let us now look closely at some of the common situations you may find yourself in and how you can encourage good behaviour so that your children will be welcome and socially accepted.

## Restaurants and cafes

Although it is perfectly reasonable for parents to want to take their children to restaurants with them, a lot of the problems experienced when dining out with young children are caused by selfish parents. If you enjoy eating out with your offspring then it is essential that you plan ahead and choose your location and timing wisely. Always remember that other diners also have the right to enjoy their meal and should not have to put up with unruly children whose table manners leave a lot to be desired.

Choose a restaurant that welcomes families and book your table for a sensible time. Yes, as parents you do have the right to enjoy some time socialising, but if you prefer to do this with your children you must remember that not everyone wants to look at them.

### *Dos and Don'ts in restaurants*

- Do choose a child-friendly place to dine
- Do book an early table so that your children are not too tired to enjoy their meal
- Do take crayons, paper, books etc. to keep young children entertained between courses
- Do insist that children display acceptable table manners
- Do ensure that children remain seated
- Do encourage children to keep noise and voices to a minimum
- Do encourage children to be polite, to say please and thank you.

- Don't allow your children to wander around – this can be dangerous when staff are waiting on tables and annoying for other diners
- Don't allow children to shout or speak loudly
- Don't allow children to fall out with each other or argue
- Don't allow children to fiddle with cutlery, glasses, plates, condiments etc.
- Don't allow children to chew with their mouths open
- Don't allow children to gobble food
- Don't allow children to make inappropriate comments about the food or service
- Don't allow your children to use their fingers to eat the food unless the food is meant to be eaten in that way.

## Table manners

Although table manners will impress no one if they are coupled with a rude, unruly child, they will go a long way to making the whole restaurant experience a pleasant one. Eating out should be an enjoyable experience for everyone – a well-deserved treat that the whole family can relate to. Teaching table manners can be as easy or as difficult as you make it. If you only care about the way your child eats when they are in public and the rest of the time you allow them to eat their meals on a tray on their lap in front of the television then you are in for a long hard slog when it comes to teaching them the importance of eating correctly. Likewise, children who are used to eating finger foods such as sandwiches, pizza and burgers for the majority of the time will find mastering a knife and fork difficult.

Ideally you will take the time to sit down as a family around the dining table at least three or four times a week. Meal times are not only good times to teach basic table manners, they are also great for catching up with one another and talking about the day's events. Many families today lead hectic lives and rarely spend time together as a family. Make meal times special for your family and encourage your children to help in preparing the meal as well as eating it.

### *Understanding the basic rules of table manners*

Children need to understand the basic rules for correct table manners which are:

- How to use a knife, fork and spoon correctly. Often young children will find it difficult to hold cutlery and it is important that you do not force them to use a knife until they are old enough to do so. A fork and a spoon, held correctly, should suffice.
- Sitting still at the table and not messing with condiments, napkins, cutlery etc.
- Sitting up straight.
- Finishing a mouthful of food before speaking.
- Saying please and thank you.
- Asking for things to be passed rather than leaning across other people or plates in order to reach them.

It is important to *show* children how things should be done correctly and *offer* suggestions rather than reprimanding them every time they do something wrong. Always remember to praise the behaviour your children are showing if you wish them to repeat it.

## The supermarket

Children absolutely hate going shopping! If at all possible when doing a big shop try to leave your toddler with someone you trust and do the shopping alone. If you do have to take your child with you, try to engage them in the shopping experience to avoid them becoming bored and restless when they are more prone to resort to tantrums.

All children like to have some responsibility and this is possible whatever the age of your child. You could put them in charge of the shopping list, if they can read, and get them to say what you need and tick items off as and when you find them. Younger children can be asked to look out for certain foods (their favourites). You could pass the groceries to your child and request that they place them carefully in the trolley (they may well toss them over their shoulder when you aren't looking but what's a few bruised apples if it keeps them happy?).

## The park

How can a child misbehave in the park, I hear you ask? Well, unfortunately they can! Despite the open air, playground apparatus and space to run around, you will still get a child who insists on running along park benches with muddy wellington boots on, standing on the swings or running through flower beds. It is important to remember that, just as you and your family enjoy the park, so too do many other people and their enjoyment of the flowers and a clean seat to rest on should not be taken from them by unruly children.

## Public transport

Whether you are travelling by bus, train, tube, boat or aeroplane, your children need to know that they must be polite and courteous to the other people using the same method of transport. It seems a long time since children were requested to give up their seat on a full bus or train when an adult was standing, but why not pleasantly surprise someone and ask your child to make room for someone who is less able to stand than they are? Make sure that your children do not drop litter on public transport and that they refrain from putting their feet on the seats.

## The streets

Children should be taught how to act responsibly in the street. They should not drop litter, be loud or run along crowded pavements. Ensure that children know how to be courteous to other pedestrians and that they do not push past people.

## Temper tantrums

This is when children *really* test your patience and push the boundaries simply because they think they can get away with it. Shock them – refuse to give in and let the tantrum take its course. It is highly likely that it will only last five or ten minutes (though admittedly this can feel like five or ten hours) as your child will either realise that their behaviour is having no affect on you whatsoever or they have run out of steam.

Giving in for a quiet life is the worst possible thing you can do. It may appease your child on this occasion but what will you do tomorrow or the next day when they resort to the same kind of behaviour in order to get their own way? If you give in now you may as well just give up altogether, refuse to show any kind of discipline and let your child do just as they please because this is the message you will be sending out. You will effectively be telling your child 'I don't want you to do that but if you scream loud enough and get as much negative attention as possible you may win me over.'

### Why do children resort to temper tantrums?

Many young children resort to tantrums as a means of getting their own way. They wrongly believe that throwing themselves on the floor, lashing out, screaming and shouting will have the desired effect. Tantrums will become common practice for children if they think they will win. The best way of dealing with a tantrum is to ignore it. Stick to your rules despite the child's behaviour and never be tempted to give in just to avoid a tantrum.

Around 50 per cent of all two year olds have tantrums on a regular basis. Tantrums usually occur in the presence of a parent or carer. Children rarely resort to tantrums in a playgroup, nursery or school environment. The main cause of tantrums is frustration and the main need for them is for attention. The best methods for dealing with tantrums are:

- Distract or divert the child
- Ignore the behaviour

- Walk away from the child.

Of course these methods are not always possible. For example, if you are in a public place it will not be an option to walk away from the child and in cases like this you should:

- Hold the child
- Reassure the child
- Offer hugs and cuddles.

But *do not* give in!

Remember that tantrums can be a frightening experience for a child. When a child is experiencing a tantrum you should never:

- Smack them
- Shake them
- Handle them roughly.

All of the above can be harmful to the child. When the tantrum is over it is important to talk to the child. Encourage them to talk about their feelings and offer reassurance in order to discourage a repeat of the behaviour.

# 7 Encouraging positive behaviour

It is all well and good knowing what type of behaviour *you* would like to see your child display, but are *they* aware of the kind of behaviour which pleases you? Or do you, as a parent, simply expect your child to know intuitively how to behave? If you think that children should know how to behave instinctively then you are in for a big shock! It is just as, if not more, important to encourage positive behaviour in your child as it is to reprimand them for displaying inappropriate behaviour. Make them feel proud of their achievements when they have behaved well and resisted the urge to throw a tantrum; let them know how proud you are of them and they will actually want to repeat the behaviour which has made you happy.

## Building a framework

Building a framework for encouraging positive behaviour is absolutely essential if your child is to understand exactly what is expected of them. Refrain from setting unrealistic targets and, if possible, work with your child to build a framework so that they will understand the reasoning behind the rules you have imposed.

Your 'house rules' are likely to be based around the things which are important to *your* children and which matter to *you*. Therefore no two families' house rules will be the same because, what matters to one family may be irrelevant to another and vice versa.

## Considering your priorities

Before you are able to build an appropriate framework for managing your own children's behaviour it is vital that you think carefully about what you personally consider important. For example, your main priority, as with most parents, may be to keep your children safe. Therefore some of your house rules will be made with this crucial factor at the forefront of your mind. Although it is not necessary for parents to actually write down a framework for managing their children's behaviour as would be expected in a nursery or school environment, it can sometimes help to put things into perspective if you jot down the issues which are important to you so that you can look closely at exactly what you feel you need to achieve from the house rules you have in place. (See Chapter 5 for a list of things to consider once you have set your rules.)

The list below gives a few examples of some of the issues you may like to consider when making your own house rules however, as mentioned earlier, every household will have different views and opinions and their house rules *must* reflect these.

- Young children are not allowed in the kitchen without adult supervision
- Young children are not allowed to venture outside of the garden without supervision
- No swearing is allowed
- Shoes are to be taken off at the door
- Respect is to be shown by everyone.

Other house rules might include requesting your children to carry out simple tasks such as:

- Making their bed
- Keeping their bedroom tidy

- Helping with the household chores
- Taking the dog for a walk.

## Helping children to understand why you have rules

Whether your household has one or two rules or dozens of rules is actually irrelevant providing everyone understands them. Your child may not agree to your rules and it will be necessary to explain to them why the rules are in place. For example if your eight year old is not allowed outside of the garden without adult supervision, they need to know that this is for their own safety and not because you are hell-bent on spoiling their fun! When children understand that you have their wellbeing in mind and that your rules are there to protect them, they will find them easier to accept.

Some rules will rarely need to be implemented as your children will learn to do things as a matter of habit after a time. For example, if you do not want outdoor shoes worn inside, insisting that your child takes their shoes off at the door from a young age will be one rule that will become a way of life rather than something which needs careful consideration.

## Adapting rules over time

Just as children are changing all the time, house rules need to be flexible. They need to take into account your child's age and growing independence. Allow your children freedom depending on their age and maturity but never be afraid of saying 'no' to something which you do not feel comfortable about. Setting times for teenagers to be home by is not cramping their style or being a kill joy, it is showing concern and protection towards your child and eliminating a sleepless night for you when you are waiting up for them to arrive home.

For children to feel safe and secure and to know what is expected of them they need to know that the rules will be consistent. There is no point in teaching your child a set of house rules when, once they have mastered them, you decide to change them.

## Establishing a framework effectively

It is important to establish a framework for behaviour early on in your child's life so that they grow up understanding what is expected of them. The tips below will help you to establish your framework effectively:

- Always praise your children when they have followed certain rules to show your appreciation and to encourage them to continue behaving well.
- Make sure that your children understand what will happen if they break the rules you have set.
- Always speak to your children in simple, clear language that they can understand. Give clear instructions so as not to confuse your children and tell them exactly what it is you expect of them.
- Remind children regularly of your house rules to keep them fresh in their minds. Often young children forget the rules rather than deliberately break them.
- Take the time to explain why you have certain rules. If your child understands why the rules are in place they are much more likely to remember them and respond positively to them.

# Understanding what motivates young children

Why do some children seem to act like little angels whilst others seem hell bent on driving us to distraction with their endless antics and unacceptable behaviour? Well firstly let's get one thing clear – no child is an angel. It is human nature for children, and sometimes adults, to push the boundaries of acceptable behaviour at some point. We all like our own way and if we thought we could get it by throwing a hissy fit every now and again how many of us wouldn't?

Children are cunning little creatures and learn very quickly how to manipulate the adults around them to get what they want. Many of us will have experienced our children, having been denied something, going directly to the other parent with the same request in the hope that mummy or daddy will be more accommodating. Sometimes this has probably worked in the child's favour, which is why they will carry on doing it. It is important however that parents work together and back one another up on important issues.

In order to understand what motivates young children we first need to look at how their needs can affect their behaviour. To be able to develop effective ways for managing behaviour it is paramount that we understand a child's needs, after their basic physiological needs to survive i.e. food, shelter, warmth and rest have been met, which are:

- To remain safe
- To feel loved, valued and respected
- To belong
- To reach their full potential.

The four main points listed above, when applied to a child, will help to shape and motivate them.

## To remain safe

Parents need to know how to keep their children safe both inside and outside the home. They need to teach their children about potential dangers and encourage them to stay alert to potential hazards. Children need to be taught how to identify, eliminate and avoid risks.

## To feel loved, valued and respected

All children need to be loved for who they are. Parents need to be kind, considerate and patient. They need to show their children that they love and respect them by listening attentively to what they have to say. Children should never be ridiculed or compared unfavourably to someone else.

### To belong

In order for a child to gain confidence and competence they need to feel as if they belong. If they are valued and respected within their own family setup, with their needs, views and opinions taken seriously, they will gain the confidence needed to forge friendships outside of the home environment and gain a sense of belonging within the community as a whole.

### To reach their full potential

The way in which you, as a parent, treat your child will determine whether or not they consider themselves worthy of having dreams they can fulfil. I believe that children should be taught that they are as capable as anyone else to achieve the dreams they have. Thousands of six year olds may dream of being pop singers and, although very few will end up realising their dream (probably because as they grow older their dream will change), it is still not acceptable for parents to laugh at their hopes or ridicule their fantasy. With ambition, encouragement, love and support it is unlikely that a child is unable to reach any realistic goal they set for themselves.

Having dreams is essential for a child to be motivated. How many of us set ourselves goals which, once achieved, result in us rewarding ourselves? You may be on a diet, for example, and, once you have achieved your target weight, you have promised yourself a new outfit. The new outfit is the motivation you need to help you to count the calories and lose the weight. Many children can be motivated through simple praise, love, patience and understanding.

## Empowerment

If we think carefully about what we would really like for our children in terms of behaviour management many parents would say that they would like their children to learn how to:

- Show a willingness to behave because they *want* to rather because they *have* to.

- Compromise so that they can behave in a way which is both acceptable to themselves and to the society in which we live.

Empowerment is all about helping children to develop confidence and positive self-esteem in order for them to be able to manage their own behaviour in a socially acceptable manner. As a parent you can help to empower your child by offering them opportunities to make choices for themselves. The choices you allow your child to make will, of course, depend on their age and level of understanding. For example, a toddler can be empowered by asking them what they would like to play with, giving them perhaps two or three choices, instead of telling them what they can or cannot do. An older child may be allowed to choose their own clothes or asked to decide what they would like for dinner.

## Giving your child responsibility

Empowerment helps a child to feel responsible. This responsibility in turn helps the child feel motivated and inwardly rewarded. They are proud of themselves for gaining the respect of the adult who has shown their respect by allowing for choices. Giving a child the opportunity to be in control of the situation, work things out for themselves and choose for themselves is a way of empowering them.

## Offering suitable choices

When encouraging empowerment it is important not to offer too many choices. Young children will be confused if you say 'What would you like to play with?' This opens up a huge variety of activities which could make the child feel overwhelmed. Instead say something like 'Would you like to play with your farm or the garage?' This narrows the choice down dramatically whilst still allowing the child freedom of choice. Older children can, of course, be offered a wider choice and should be allowed to make more complex decisions. Providing children with simple tasks, suitable to their age and level of understanding, also helps a child to feel empowered.

## Using rewards to reinforce positive behaviour

It is important that we do not mistake using rewards with bribing our children. It is possible to reinforce positive behaviour that we would like our children to repeat with praise and rewards. This method works well with most children. Think about your own behaviour. It can be particularly pleasing when someone congratulates you on a job well done and whilst you may not actually receive a 'reward' the praise alone can be sufficient to boost your confidence and make you want to repeat the experience. Children need to be treated in much the same way. Boosting their confidence with praise can be very effective.

Praise should be used frequently when caring for young children although rewards can also be used when your child has shown particularly pleasing behaviour. It is important to remember that, whilst praise should be forthcoming whenever it is due, rewards should be kept to a minimum.

## Things to remember when using praise and rewards

- ✓ Praise your child frequently. Showing your child that you are pleased with their behaviour will help to encourage positive behaviour.
- ✓ Explain to your child why they are being rewarded or praised. Aim to praise your child and give any rewards at the *actual* time they are displaying positive behaviour and reiterate why they are being praised.
- ✓ Make sure that you choose your rewards carefully. A full bag of sweets used as a reward for when your child has helped to put their toys away would be inappropriate, however one sweet or a sticker would be ideal.

### Choosing appropriate rewards

Although it is easy to praise your child when they are showing signs of appropriate behaviour, it is often more difficult to choose appropriate rewards. It is also important to avoid jealousy amongst siblings who may perhaps find it more difficult to earn rewards, particularly if they are much younger. Some of the rewards you may opt for could include the following.

### Sweets

Rewards do not necessarily have to be sweets. Some parents do not like their children to have sweets and therefore by giving sweets as a reward for good behaviour you may unintentionally give the wrong message to your child. Being allowed something which is usually off limits is not an effective way of promoting positive behaviour. Try substituting sweets for healthy food such as grapes, carrot sticks, celery, raisins or other special treats your child may like.

### Small toys

Rewarding your child with a small toy should not be regular practice as, apart from the expense, they may come to expect a gift every time they have behaved well. Children should be encouraged to behave well because they *want* to, not simply because they are aiming for a present. Small toys could however be useful to reward a child's behaviour if they have behaved well during times of adversity or if their routine has been particularly disrupted, for example, in the case of the birth of a new baby.

### Stickers

Stickers are an excellent way of rewarding a child for specific behaviour and can easily take the place of sweets/fruit. Stickers can be awarded directly to the child and can be particularly useful if you are trying to get your child to achieve a certain goal such as dressing themselves, using the potty or keeping their bedroom tidy. Each time your child has successfully carried out the task they would receive a sticker. Children love to see tangible evidence of their achievements and to have their good behaviour acknowledged; stickers provide an excellent way of doing this and many parents purchase or make charts for their children to display their stickers on.

# Responding to unwanted behaviour

## What triggers unwanted behaviour?

Before we can successfully respond to the unwanted behaviour shown by children from time to time, we first need to understand their behaviour and have some idea of the type of things which may trigger unacceptable behaviour.

### Temperament

We looked at some of the basic factors which a child may experience and which may influence their behaviour in Chapter 3. However, it is also important to bear in mind that although much behaviour is learnt there are also some behaviours which the child is born with, such as their disposition and temperament. All children are individuals and their own genetic makeup is what makes them unique.

Many people believe that a person's personality is inherited, however that would then mean that a child born to very shy parents would themselves be prone to shyness and, likewise a child whose parents were outgoing and sociable would produce children who were the life and soul of the party. This is not always the case of course and often shy parents can produce sociable, outgoing children and vice versa.

### Family

One of the most powerful influences, on a child's behaviour is that of the family. Children are usually born into a family which will rear them, teach them, love them and nurture them. It is easy to see therefore how the family influences the way in which a child grows up.

### Stage of development

In addition to the common triggers of unacceptable behaviour such as tiredness, boredom, illness and so on, it is also important to bear in mind the child's age and stage of development. For example, if communication has not yet been mastered adequately, a young child may resort to unwanted behaviour through frustration if they are unable to make themselves understood. Although these factors are not excuses, they are *triggers* of unacceptable behaviour that must not be discounted.

## Dealing with unwanted behaviour

When dealing with types of unwanted behaviour it is important to consider ways in which behaviour can be kept in check. Some of these methods, such as smacking, are very controversial.

## Smacking

The great smacking debate is something which has been discussed for many years and by literally millions of people. It is a sensitive subject which has seen a huge divide in opinion. People feel very strongly about smacking – they are either in complete acceptance of it or they are firmly against it. Many parents think that a short, sharp slap is a good deterrent which shows children who is in control and puts a stop to unwanted behaviour. Others believe the complete opposite and would even go as far as to say that smacking is a form of abuse.

Whatever your own personal opinions on smacking one thing is certain: smacking allows the parent to let off steam. Whether this is a good thing or a bad one I will let you decide for yourself.

It is probably true to say that most parents have resorted to, or at the very least thought about, smacking their children – children can and will try the patience of a saint – and it is worth pointing out that there are both pros and cons for resorting to punishing a child in this way, whatever your personal opinions of smacking are.

## Using smacking as a punishment: the pros

- It provides a short, sharp shock intended to get the child's attention.
- It can show the child that the adult is in charge.
- It can be a way of showing extreme disapproval.
- It can be used to prevent a child doing something dangerous (a slap of the hand to prevent a child from touching a hot surface for example).
- It can be an instant deterrent.

## Using smacking as a punishment: the cons

- It can give children the wrong message. It may lead children to believe that smacking is an acceptable way of dealing with certain situations and may result in the child themselves resorting to smacking.
- As the child is much smaller than the adult it can be seen as a form of abuse or bullying.
- It may prevent a child from exploring their environment for fear of a repercussion in the form of a smack if they touch something which is out of bounds.
- It allows the adult to vent their anger and may, in some circumstances, spiral out of control. If the adult loses their temper a single smack may lead to a serious beating.

- A child who is smacked often may become immune to this kind of punishment after a while. This may lead the parent to find alternative methods, such as using a belt or slipper, which could lead to serious injury.
- It can be difficult to decide which kind of behaviour 'deserves' a smack and which can be controlled in other ways. Over use of smacking could be the result.

Many people today, particularly the older generation, firmly believe that children were better behaved in 'their day' when children were often disciplined with the use of smacking. School children were subjected to the cane for misbehaving whereas now, despite teachers being sworn at and physically threatened or even harmed, this form of punishment is against the law.

## Shouting

It is human nature to lose your temper sometimes, although of course how often this happens will vary from individual to individual and will most probably depend on how many children you have and how they behave. The bad news, I am afraid, is that shouting very rarely works as a form of behaviour management. True, it allows the adults to let off steam and may be seen by many as preferable to inflicting a smack on the child but, as with physical punishment, it gives off the completely wrong messages and actually tells children that you, the parent, have lost control of the situation. This is never a good idea!

### Losing impact

Shouting, if used regularly, will cease to have any impact whatsoever on the behaviour management of your children. It will, however, quite probably raise the volume of the entire household as everyone will struggle to compete with the shouting. This will result in an accumulation of voices so loud that no-one can actually hear or concentrate on what is being said.

Having worked with children of all ages for many years and brought up two children of my own I have come to the conclusion that shouting is in no way a suitable method of behaviour management. The result is a sore throat and very little else.

Shouting, in my opinion, does not work for several reasons:

- It shows that you have lost control.
- It never diffuses a problem it simply adds to what is already a fraught situation.
- It can result in confrontations – often children will shout back or argue.
- It is more likely to frighten a child than encourage them to take notice and listen to what you have to say.
- It sets children a bad example.

It is far better to speak in a controlled, firm voice and state exactly what it is you are not happy about with regards to your child's behaviour than to fly off the handle and rant and rave at them.

## Using body language

We can say as much through our body language as we can with the spoken word. It is for this reason that we should be aware of our own body language and what exactly we are 'saying'. For example a look of disapproval is often all that is needed to stop a child from acting in a certain way. This can be by raising an eyebrow or giving a stern look.

In much the same way the manner in which we carry our bodies will also convey certain messages to children.

### Approving body language

- Smiling, grinning and laughing
- Eyes wide, watching interestedly

- Arms outstretched inviting a hug
- Kissing
- Cuddles and hugs
- Gently touching

### Disapproving body language

- Stern look
- Raised eyebrow
- Frowning
- Arms folded
- Hands on hips
- Raised hand

### Emphasising your message

Using several forms of body language at once, for example a stern look coupled with crossed arms, or a broad smile with outstretched arms, will increase the power of the non-verbal communication you are sending out to your child.

## Applying punishments and sanctions

So, if you have decided that smacking is not for you and you do not wish to use this form of punishment, then what other means do you have left to ensure that your child sticks to the rules and behaves in a socially acceptable manner? Well for a start smacking is by no means the only way of managing a child's behaviour and if you have decided that this is not for you that does not let you off the hook in dealing with your child's negative behaviour.

## Using preventative strategies

The best way to deal with unwanted behaviour is to use positive, preventative strategies. By anticipating potential sources of danger or conflict and eliminating them, together with ensuring that children are well supervised and have interesting activities, you will be well on the way to creating a positive environment for children to thrive in. The following list shows several ways in which you can intervene should a child be displaying inappropriate behaviour.

## Methods of intervening when a child displays unwanted behaviour

- A firm 'no'
- Eye contact and facial expressions
- Explanation of what will happen if the child persists in showing unwanted behaviour
- Removal of the toy or equipment
- Time out.

Let us now look at these methods in more detail.

### *A firm 'no'*

Most children will respond well to this verbal expression and will usually understand its meaning from a very early age. For this command to work well though, it must be used sparingly. When you have told a child 'no', it is important that you explain why they are not allowed to do it and that you mean what you say. Never allow children to continue showing unacceptable behaviour or persuade you to change your mind. Saying 'no' coupled with the appropriate tone of voice and facial expression can be very effective.

### *Eye contact and facial expressions*

Sometimes a child who is aware of what is expected of them may test the boundaries by trying to over-step them. In these cases quite often a simple look is sufficient to let them know that their behaviour is unacceptable. Eye contact should be used with the appropriate facial expression, i.e. a look of disapproval.

### *Explanation of what will happen if the child persists in showing unwanted behaviour*

Children should always be made aware of the consequences of their actions. Explaining the consequences underlines the importance of the rules and sets clear boundaries. Never make idle threats. By threatening sanctions that are unjustified or cannot be carried through you will undermine your own authority and confuse the child.

### *Removal of the toy or equipment*

This should always be used as a last resort. Children should be allowed to rectify their behaviour initially, through compromise and warnings, before the toy or equipment is removed. By removing a toy or equipment before giving the child the opportunity to rectify their behaviour you will have taught them nothing. They will not know why you have taken the object away from them and will probably move on to another toy and continue with the same unwanted behaviour. For example if a child throws a toy across the room and you refuse to allow them to have it back, the child will simply pick up another toy and do the same thing. How are you going to solve this problem – by taking away all the toys?

You should say a firm 'no' initially coupled with an expression of disapproval. If the behaviour persists, and the child is old enough to understand, then an explanation should be given as to why it is not acceptable to throw toys indoors. For example, the toy may hit someone and cause injury, the toy may break something, or the toy itself may be damaged. If appropriate, try offering the child the opportunity of going outdoors to throw a ball as an alternative to throwing a toy indoors.

### *Time out*

Time out is not the same as isolation. Isolating a child is not an effective method of behaviour management, and children should never be put in a room and left alone. Time out is similar to removing toys and equipment in that it deprives the child of something they want. Time out allows both the child and the adult to calm down and take control of themselves. This method of behaviour management is particularly effective for more serious misdemeanours such as destructiveness, violence, swearing, rudeness etc. A few minutes 'time out' should be long enough to diffuse the situation.

Time out is more appropriate to older children who will respond more effectively to being removed from a situation they are having difficulty with. A child should be removed from the situation causing the problem and taken to one side. An explanation of what is unacceptable should be given, appropriate to the age and level of understanding of the child.

Time out should never be coupled with using a 'naughty chair' or 'naughty corner'. These are forms of humiliation and they will not help to calm a child down but will merely encourage anger and resentment. Time out is not a punishment, it is a way of getting a child to calm down and to step back from the problem. Offer reassurance and sympathy when talking to the child and remember that emotions are very powerful and are often difficult for a child to control.

## Ignoring the behaviour

Whenever possible, ignore a child who is exhibiting unacceptable behaviour. They are usually acting this way to gain attention and the best thing you can do is to refuse them the attention they are seeking whilst they are behaving in an unacceptable manner. By giving a badly behaved child your attention you have effectively given them what they want. The attention they receive may not necessarily be desirable but it is attention nonetheless. If possible, walk away from the child or busy yourself with a task which means you are taking no notice of what the child is doing. If a child sees that their unacceptable behaviour is having no affect on you they will quickly tire and move onto something else.

A child who is acting disruptively, for example, is usually doing so for a reaction. He may be looking to shock you, annoy you, upset you or anger you. By ignoring this behaviour you are refusing to allow him to control the situation and he will quickly realise that his efforts are in vain. Obviously there are times when ignoring the behaviour or walking away from the child will not be an option, for example if their behaviour poses a danger to themselves or someone else or if you are in a public place at the time. This is when distraction should be used.

## Distraction

Distraction can be a very useful form of behaviour management when other methods fail. A child who is causing a scene because she wants a toy that someone else is playing with can have her behaviour successfully managed by the use of distraction. Failure to get what she wants could result in a tantrum, however by distracting her and getting her interested in another toy you can help to diffuse the situation and avert the problem.

## Play therapy

Play therapy is an ideal way for children to act out situations that cause anxiety and stress and which may lead to problems with behaviour. It provides a child with a way to release strong emotions in a safe environment and in a non-threatening way.

Play therapy can be used in a number of ways such as:

- Physical play. Kicking a ball about outside or running around a playground are good ways of releasing pent-up energy which may turn into anger and frustration.

- Play dough and clay are good for kneading when feelings of frustration are threatening to take over.
- Role play, such as hospital and school, is good for expressing anxiety and fear which a child may experience before a hospital appointment or a change in schools for example.
- Books are an excellent source of information on a huge scale of topics from bereavement, visiting the dentist, dealing with a new baby, moving house, starting school etc. and parents are well advised to think about tackling issues which may be relevant to their child in this way. Sharing stories can help a child to understand issues which may otherwise be difficult for parents to explain.

**SIX EFFECTIVE STEPS TO PROMOTE POSITIVE BEHAVIOUR IN CHILDREN**

✓ Be consistent – mean what you say!
✓ Be a good role model – children copy what they see and hear.
✓ Use praise and rewards – children love to please.
✓ Ignore bad behaviour whenever possible.
✓ Use 'time out' to diffuse the situation.
✓ Apply sanctions whenever necessary.

Whatever strategy you use it is important to make children aware that it is the behaviour they are displaying that you do not like and not the child themselves.

# Exploring feelings

I often wonder how many of us considered ourselves to be perfect parenting material *before* we had actually had children of our own. It is doubtful that I am the only person who has watched from the sidelines as other parents try to discipline their children, thinking smugly how I could do a much better job. I suppose I considered myself an expert on children before actually becoming a mother myself.

Now that I am a mother I could never be so blasé about such matters as I know, despite having hands-on experience, I am still no expert when it comes to parenting issues. This is because no two children are alike and what works with one child may not work with another. No parent can truly say that they have all the answers.

One thing I have learned over the years, whilst working with children and being a mother to my own children, is that behaviour happens *for a reason*. If a child misbehaves they do so for a reason, if they cooperate they do so for a reason. Just as we, as adults, respond well to kindness, so too will your child. It is absolutely paramount that parents are in tune with the way their children feel and that they understand how their child's emotions can affect the way in which they behave.

## Understanding how your child is feeling

It is probably true to say that most parents do not even consider their child's feelings let alone accept them. Children, like adults, deserve explanations and their feelings should be considered and taken into account. It is my opinion that if a child feels loved and valued, in the vast majority of cases, they will behave in an acceptable manner. So, how do we ensure that our children are loved and valued? We *understand* and *accept* their feelings!

## Common ways parents 'deny' their child's feelings

Parents are often guilty of denying their children's feelings when faced with problems or situations they are uncomfortable with or which they feel unable to change. The following list gives some examples of a statement that a child may make, that the parent subsequently denies.

1. Child says 'I hate school – I'm not going again.'
2. Child says 'I'm not eating that dinner – it's disgusting!'
3. Child says 'My shoes are hurting, I can't walk any further.'
4. Child says 'I'm not going to bed, I'm not tired.'
5. Child says 'I can't get dressed this morning, my head is hurting and I feel sick.'

I wonder how many parents when faced with these kinds of scenarios would automatically be on the defensive. Let us look at the five statements again and consider some of the responses which parents are likely to give.

1. If your child tells you that they hate school and are not going again, how would you respond? Would you:
   — Tell them to stop being silly?
   — Tell them that they have to go again?
   — Tell them that they have just had a bad day but now it's over?

   OR would you acknowledge your child's feelings and try to find out why they feel this way?

2. If your child tells you that they are not eating their dinner because it is disgusting, how would you respond? Would you:
   — Tell them they couldn't leave the table until they had cleared their plate?
   — Say 'Of course you like it – you've eaten it before.'
   — Begin to tell them how long it has taken you to prepare the meal and how ungrateful they are being?

   OR would you acknowledge the fact that your child may simply not be hungry or that their tastes have changed?

3. If your child tells you that their shoes are hurting and they can't walk any further would you:
   — Say 'Don't be silly, they can't be hurting you've only had them a couple of months.'
   — Say 'You're just being lazy.'
   — Say 'You're only complaining because you want me to carry you!'

   OR would you acknowledge that your child may be tired or that their shoes have rubbed their feet?

4. If your child tells you they are not tired and that they don't want to go to bed would you:
   — Say 'Of course you're tired – it's eight o'clock.'
   — Say 'You *are* tired – look you can hardly keep your eyes open!'

   OR would you acknowledge that, on this particular day, your child is not feeling as sleepy as they usually are?

5. If your child told you that they couldn't get dressed because they had a headache and felt sick would you:
   — Say 'We are late: stop messing around and get dressed.'
   — Say 'You haven't got a headache and you are not sick, you just don't want to go to school!'

   OR would you acknowledge your child's complaint and investigate it?

I am sure, when most of you read these statements, you will be adamant that you would always acknowledge what your child says and take their feelings into account. However, I would be very doubtful if some of you have not, at some point, been guilty of responding to your child with a 'denial' of some sort.

Listening to and accepting your child's feelings does not meant that you have to 'give in' to them and allow them complete freedom. For example, in the case of a child who says they are not tired and that they don't want to go to bed; by accepting what they say you do not have to allow them to stay up later than usual, this could of course be detrimental if they have to go to school the next morning. However you should acknowledge what they are saying rather than telling them how they feel! You could try responding to this statement by saying something along the lines of 'Maybe you don't feel very sleepy just yet but, by the time you have brushed your teeth and listened to a story, you may feel differently.' Follow this up with an explanation of why your child needs their sleep.

## Accepting your child's feelings

When your child tells you how they are feeling you must always give them your *full* attention. Listening half-heartedly will prevent them from opening up to you in the future. Refrain from questioning their feelings or offering advice immediately – try to acknowledge what they have to say first. Talk your child's feelings through with them and explore together possible explanations or reasons for the way they are feeling instead of denying their emotions.

Children need a sense of identity, to know who they are and what is expected of them. They need to develop positive self-esteem and build on their confidence if they are to develop into well-rounded, sociable adults.

# Showing feelings and emotions

Children develop a sense of identity, known as self-concept, during the first year of their life. Their sense of identity increases and becomes more stable as they learn how to develop socially and make friends. In order for a child to develop a positive sense of identity they need help and encouragement from their parents and the other adults around them to understand:

- How to accept themselves
- How to like themselves
- How to respect themselves
- How to develop a positive self-image
- How and why they exist
- Who they are
- How to develop self-esteem
- How to develop skills which will enable them to care for themselves.

## Encouraging a positive sense of identity

There are a number of ways which you, the parent, can help and encourage your child to develop a positive sense of identity:

- Develop strong attachments with your child starting from the very early days of their life.
- Show love and affection towards your child in order for them to develop socially.
- Accept your child for who they are and what they can do without setting unrealistic targets or pushing them before they are ready.
- Respect and value your child so that they, in turn, will learn how to respect and value themselves.
- Ensure, when they have not behaved in an appropriate manner, that it is your child's behaviour you do not like and not your child.

Children who learn to value and respect themselves will develop a positive self-concept and good self-esteem. With these important life skills they will be in a good position to show and handle their feelings and emotions.

## Overwhelming feelings

It is important to remember that a child's feelings and emotions will often be very strong and can, at times, be quite frightening for them. They may quickly become overwhelmed by their feelings and emotions which are often changeable and confusing. Children may feel a whole array of feelings as widely differing as:

- temper tantrums
- anger and rage
- sadness and crying

- jealousy
- intense joy and happiness.

Often very young children, who have not yet mastered articulation, may struggle to put their feelings into words and the added frustration of being unable to tell someone how they are feeling may increase the emotions they are experiencing. Often a child will 'hit out' because they are frustrated. If, for example, someone is hurting them and they are unable to convey what they want to say through speech i.e., 'Stop that, you are hurting me!' they will simply hit back. Children who bite often do so through this type of frustration as they lack the communication skills required to let their feelings be adequately understood.

### Supporting your child

Children need time, space and lots of adult support in order for them to learn to accept, express and deal with their emotions. It is important that you show your child patience when they are dealing with their feelings so that they will learn how to negotiate with others and to build positive friendships.

## Raising a child's self-esteem

For a child to develop self-esteem they need love and security. They also need to feel trusted and be able to trust those around them. Children will not learn to love and trust overnight. This is something that will develop over years, but only if they experience this kind of behaviour for themselves. A child who has never been shown love or felt trusted will struggle to show affection and put their trust in others. In addition to ensuring that your child feels loved, valued and trusted there are a number of other ways in which parents and other adults can raise a child's self-esteem.

- **Encourage your child.** Children, like adults, learn by their mistakes. Despite the fact that your child may attempt to do something and fail you should always be there with encouragement. Never scold your child for having a go at something even if the outcome is not what you expected. Ridiculing a child, or berating them for have attempted something and failed, will put them off trying new experiences in the future.

- **Provide consistent care.** Children need to know that their parents and other important adults in their lives believe in them and are there for them. As a parent it is your responsibility to make time for your child and not simply fit them in around work and other commitments.
- **Provide positive role models.** By showing children what is expected of them, using positive role models, you will influence them greatly. Young children often look up to the adults around them and imitate their behaviour. Showing respect, trust and honesty will show children how to behave in this way themselves. Try to be a good role model at all times and refrain from portraying images of self-doubt or depression when your children are around.
- **Provide children with clear, consistent boundaries** so that they are aware of what is expected of them and do not become confused or resort to testing the boundaries.
- **Help your child to be a success** by avoiding setting unrealistically high expectations of what you would like them to achieve.
- **Appreciate your child's efforts** when they have attempted something for the first time. Remember the effort should be seen as more important than the result if you are to boost a child's confidence and self-esteem.
- **Allow your child the freedom to make choices for themselves.** Always being told exactly what to do will demean a child and lower their confidence. Giving a child choices and allowing them to make decisions based on their age and stage of development will greatly encourage their ability and boost self-esteem and give them a feeling of self-worth and competence.
- **Help your child to find something they are good at.** All children, regardless of their learning or physical ability, are good at something and it is important to encourage a child to find their niche – something they know they can excel at and which will raise their confidence. They may have a particular aptitude for music or a sporting prowess, or it may be something as simple as being organised, helpful or caring. Finding the one thing that a child is

really good at will lead them to look for other things they are capable of doing confidently. As a parent it is your job to find the things your child can excel at.

## Encouraging self-respect in children

When a child has begun to feel as if they belong in their own immediate family they generally wish to expand their social network and become more widely accepted by others.

For a child to feel accepted, loved and respected they first need to develop these feeling towards themselves. Children who are brought up in an environment where their efforts and achievements go unnoticed will fail to thrive because their confidence will take a battering. Their self-esteem will not be raised as they fear rejection and experience feelings of inadequacy.

Those children whose parents take an active interest in what they do, and offer help and encouragement will develop positive self-esteem and will quickly become competent and capable. A child whose efforts are praised is much more likely to attempt to learn other skills and will be much more motivated. However it is important that parents understand that they need to have realistic views of what their child can achieve as repeated failure may result in the child feeling frustrated, angry and dissatisfied; they may even decide not to attempt new tasks for fear of failure again.

### Allowing your child control

Children also need to have some kind of control over the tasks they attempt. A parent who consistently does things for their child reduces the chances of the child themselves trying out new skills and will undermine the child's ability and confidence. For example, a father who always ties his son's shoelaces 'because it is quicker' or a mother who refuses to allow her toddler to attempt to feed themselves because 'they make a mess' is effectively denying their child any control over the situation and this can lead to frustration.

## Building confidence

When a child is allowed some control over things they begin to develop a feeling of confidence and prestige and experience a sense of usefulness and worthiness all of which add to their self-respect. Occasionally a child who is unable to gain recognition and who fails to satisfy their need for self-esteem in an appropriate manner may resort to tantrums or destructive behaviour mainly through frustration, falsely believing that they may gain recognition this way because they have failed to achieve it through constructive or appropriate methods.

A child's social and emotional development is closely linked to all other areas of their development and cannot therefore be separated. Children who have difficulty communicating, for example, will have less ability to socialise and make friends, which will in turn lead to them feeling undervalued or insecure.

Developing self-respect in children needs patience and understanding. In many ways achieving self-respect can be a vicious circle. Before commanding respect a person needs to show respect; before showing respect for others we must first respect ourselves.

## Giving a child responsibility

One of the easiest and most beneficial ways of helping a child to develop self-respect is to allow them responsibility for themselves. Of course, the amount of responsibility you allow your child will be dependent on their age and stage of development. No child should be given responsibilities which may put them in danger or cause them harm, but it is important to remember that *all* children can be given some degree of responsibility no matter how small it may appear. A three year old may be encouraged to be responsible for helping to put their toys away whilst a teenager may be responsible for tidying their room or doing the washing up.

## Acknowledging your child's individuality

It is inevitable, at some point, that you will look at your child and they will remind you of someone. This may or may not be a good thing. They may remind you of yourself or they may remind you of your partner. They may even remind you of someone you prefer not to think about. This can be very difficult in situations where parents are separated or divorced and the child becomes a constant reminder of a person's ex. It is vital that you accept your child and learn to appreciate *all* their qualities even those that remind you of someone else. Your child is unique and you need to acknowledge and praise their individuality.

Sometimes you may look at your child for some clue as to how they could possibly be yours. You may try, and fail, to see any similarities between yourself and your offspring. You may, at times, feel as if you have absolutely nothing in common with your child and cannot understand what makes them tick. Your child is not a clone of you nor should you expect or want them to be. Your child is an individual with their own identity.

As your child gets older you may well feel the differences between you becoming more significant. Often parents of teenagers worry that they are 'losing' their children. This is not the case; your teenager is growing up and becoming an adult in their own right. Rather than worry about this transition, you should embrace it and acknowledge the fact that you have brought up a well-adjusted young adult.

A good parent is one who will allow their child the freedom to express themselves and to embrace life and all that it offers. Remember parents can learn from children in just the same way as children learn from their parents if we would only allow them to teach us!

# Social skills

## How friendships are formed

Some people think that young children are incapable of forming meaningful friendships until they reach the age of around six or seven years, whilst others firmly believe that pre-school children are capable of developing strong friendships. One thing is certain though – friendships can be a great source of happiness and contentment in a child's life. A child who has difficulty relating to others may experience sadness if they are unable to forge lasting, meaningful friendships.

## Ways of encouraging your child to relate to others

There are a number of ways in which parents can encourage their child to relate to others:

- **Provide positive role models.** Parents whose children witness them being diplomatic, kind and helpful are more likely to imitate this kind of behaviour and see it as being the correct way to behave. Parents who are unco-operative and out for themselves are more likely to produce mean, self-centred children.
- **Provide the appropriate number of age-related toys and resources.** Siblings who have to share everything may find it difficult to be co-operative if they have to wait too long to play with a particular toy. Although you can't be expected to purchase multitudes of toys and indeed this can be very costly, nor should you expect three children to play with one doll – this is asking for trouble!

- **Provide your children with games and activities** which encourage cooperation, sharing and turn-taking.
- **Praise your child** when they have shown particular kindness towards another or if they have demonstrated an ability to share and take turns.

I firmly believe that all children regardless of their age and stage of development are capable of forming friendships. The nature and intensity of these friendships will, of course, change as the child gets older and becomes more mature but it is important that children understand, from an early age, the importance of making and developing friendships.

## Different stages of play

Children go through different stages of play.

- **Solitary play** – from the ages of birth to two years most children will play alone.
- **Spectator play** – from the ages of two to three years most children will enjoy watching other children play but will rarely join in.
- **Parallel play** – again from the ages of two to three years children will play alongside one another but rarely will they play together.
- **Associative play** – between the ages of three and four years children are beginning to form bonds. They may occasionally play co-operatively.

Fig. 1: **Stages of play**

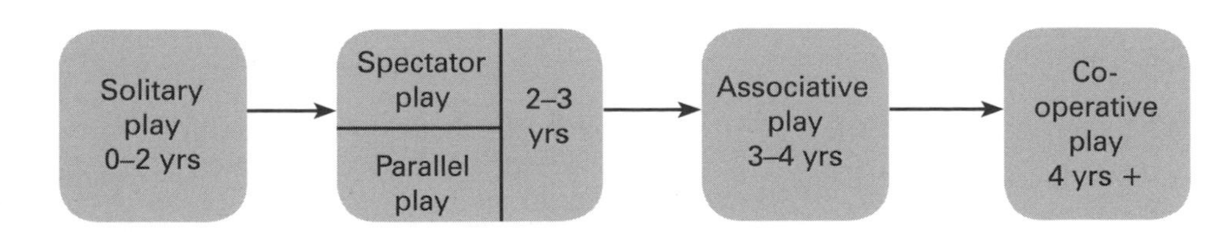

- **Co-operative play** – once a child reaches the age of four years they are usually able to play co-operatively and support one another.

## Learning to share, take turns and co-operate with one another

Learning to share, take turns and co-operate with one another can be very difficult for some children, particularly those who have no siblings or extended family. These children may never have *had* to share until they reach the pre-school, nursery or school setting.

### *Birth to four years*

It is widely believed that young children, up to the age of two years, enjoy playing side by side but, although they notice each other and the activities someone else is engaged in, it is not usually until children are aged about four years that they begin to learn how to play co-operatively and start to show a preference in whom they wish to play with. Usually children under the age of four years will not mind if they play with their own or the opposite gender. It is often the activity which engages their interest rather than the individuals involved.

### *Four to seven years*

Children between the ages of four and seven years place a great emphasis on their friendships and may often become distressed if a particular friend is not in school for some reason. As children become more able to play imaginatively together, the possibilities increase for sharing and enjoying each other's company.

### *Eight years plus*

When a child reaches the age of eight years they have usually begun to form stable friendships based on compatibility and will often choose their friends according to common interests. Between the ages of eight and eleven years friendships appear to involve the same sex and boys tend to be more prone to 'group' gatherings with girls preferring to 'couple up'.

## Changing friendships

Although some children who begin life as 'friends', perhaps through their parents, may continue their friendship into later life you should be prepared for things to change when your child gets older and becomes more mature. Remember, just because you are good friends with a particular child's mother, it is not a foregone conclusion that your children's friendships will develop in the same way.

Once a child begins school they will be mixing with a lot of new children – some they will like and some they won't. With this influx of people joining their social circle, your child may be overwhelmed with the number of new and exciting prospects these potential friends have to offer and they may even drop existing friends they have known for some time. This can have a devastating affect on the child who has been left behind in favour of a new bosom buddy. If your child is the one being overlooked, you will need to offer reassurance and work with them to overcome their feelings of despair. It is important to remember that friendships, although often deep rooted and meaningful, can also be very fragile and will often, in the case of children, fall apart. If your child is on the receiving end of a 'fall out' with friends it is important that you acknowledge their feelings and help them to get through the difficult transition they are facing.

## Popularity

Some children are more popular than others and, no matter how hard a child may try, that all-important popularity may elude them. It is not clear exactly why some children are more popular than others although it would seem that those children with good social skills are more likely to come first in the popularity stakes.

## Popular children

Popular children are likely to:

- Understand the importance of joining in a game
- Understand the importance of sharing and taking turns.

In some cases popular children are also likely to be more physically attractive than others and may be the children of financially well-off parents, putting them in the position of appearing 'attractive' in what they have to offer friends in the way of toys and material possessions.

## Unpopular children

Unpopular children are likely to:

- Be forceful and demanding, trying to take over rather than join in a game
- Be aggressive
- Be unsure how to judge people or situations and often wrongly believe that people are being hostile towards them
- Be disruptive.

## Acceptance

It appears that only a relatively few children make it to the star status of being popular, however it is important to remember that being popular is not something which is vital or indeed even necessary. What you should be striving for is for your child to be *accepted generally* in order for them to be happy and have friends.

Your child's overall development and general well-being will depend on being accepted by their peers and being a part of reciprocal relationships.

# Working together

Being accepted, getting on well with peers and having friends is an important complex process. However, preparing your child is not just about teaching them all about the skills needed for making friends though this is, of course, important. It is your child's overall general behaviour which is likely to affect the way they are seen by others and whether this behaviour is likely to affect or limit their acceptance amongst their peers. For example, a child who always appears to be in trouble or is boisterous or disruptive may find that his behaviour affects his friendships if other children do not wish to associate with him for fear of repercussions.

## Assessing your child's current social relationships

Before deciding how to help and encourage your child to make friends it may help you to understand any problems they may be experiencing by answering, honestly, a few simple questions. The questions set out below will help you to assess the extent and the quality of your child's current social relationships. These questions are particularly suited to parents with children who are attending some kind of day care session, whether this is a nursery or pre-school facility.

- Does your child speak to, and respond well with, the adults at his/her nursery or pre-school setting?
- Does your child willingly share their toys?
- Does your child wait their turn happily or under duress?
- Does your child respond positively when approached by other children?
- Does your child prefer to play alone?
- Does your child initiate play with others or wait for other children to approach them?
- Does your child find it difficult to control their temper?
- Does your child tend to take over activities or do they play co-operatively?
- Does your child regularly get into fights or disagreements?

In order for a child to develop social skills and form valuable, meaningful friendships they need to know how to work in partnership with others. Some children find making friends easy whilst others struggle to develop friendships.

## Why children find it hard to make friends

Those who find it hard to make friends may do so for a number of reasons:

- They may not have any siblings and therefore have no experience of mixing with other children.
- They may have had no opportunities to mix with other children outside of their home environment.
- They may live in an isolated area where neighbours are far and few between.
- They may be shy.
- They may have experienced bullying.
- They may lack confidence.

## Providing your child with the skills they need to mix with others

Tackling any problems which are apparent with regard to socialisation early on is the best way to help your child. By answering the questions raised above you will be able to identify any areas which may be problematic and address these immediately in order to avoid any major problems. This is often easier said than done although there are several ways in which parents can help their child to socialise, such as:

- Encourage your child to join various clubs which they may find interesting and which will enable them to meet other children with shared interests.

- Encourage your child to invite some of their fellow class mates to your house for tea and to play – this in turn may lead to the invitation being reciprocated.
- Find out whether they are being bullied (there is more about bullying in Chapter 11).
- Help to boost their confidence with lots of praise and encouragement.

Children who lack confidence will be self-conscious and will find it difficult to mix with others for fear of rejection. Unfortunately building your child's confidence is not always an easy process and they will need your encouragement and patience whilst they tackle this skill. Giving them lots of praise, in order to make them feel good about themselves, will help to boost their confidence.

### Trying not to push your child

Although many parents may worry if their child does not appear to be making lots of friends it is important to remember not to push them until they are ready. A shy, reserved child may retreat even further into their shell if forced into a situation they are not happy with. It is also worth remembering that not every child can be the life and soul of the party and, although some children are very popular and appear to have dozens of friends, others are just as happy, content and fulfilled with just one close and valued friend.

## When children fall out

Often childhood 'fall outs' are short lived and, within a day or two, the children will have made up and resumed their friendship. However, in some cases, this does not happen and the friendship may never be repaired. Parents must never underestimate the emotions experienced by a child during the breakdown of a friendship.

## Helping your child through a friendship crisis

In order to help your child through a friendship crisis you will need to:

- **Take your child seriously.** It is important that parents treat their child with respect and listen to their woes.
- **Recognise that your child is experiencing real feelings** of hurt and upset. *Never* dismiss your child's feelings or tell them to 'pull themselves together'. Telling your child to get on with things as this is all part of growing up will not help their predicament and may even force them to keep their feelings to themselves resulting in further turmoil.
- **Try to put yourself in your child's shoes.** If possible think back to a time when you experienced similar feelings and try to remember how you felt at that time.
- **Never laugh at your child's experiences** even if this is in an attempt to make light of the problem. Remember your child needs you to understand what they are going through.
- **Try to find out what has happened** as gently as possible. What actually caused the rift? Could a bit of diplomacy sort things out? Is there anything you can do to help?
- **Encourage your child to move on.** If there is no chance of the friendship being mended then your child needs to make new friends and the sooner they are able to do this, the sooner they will be able to move on.

# Controlling emotions

Emotions are experienced by us all – they are part of being human. However we need to control our emotions in order to become socially acceptable. Imagine how you would feel if you saw an adult throwing themselves on the floor of the supermarket and having a tantrum! A child's emotions can be very strong and, at times, quite frightening. They can vary from deep despair to euphoria within a matter of minutes. These kinds of mood swings can be quite worrying for parents if they do not understand the reasons behind them.

Some of the feelings which children may experience include:

- happiness
- euphoria
- sadness
- fear
- joy
- aggression
- jealousy
- tension
- anger.

They may show their feelings and emotions through:

- Being quiet
- Being boisterous and noisy
- Appearing thoughtful.

It is important for parents to:

- Acknowledge their child's feelings and emotions
- Encourage the expression of their feelings and emotions in a safe environment
- Deal with these feelings.

Although it is possible for adults to moderate their feelings and put things into perspective, this is rarely the case with young children who tend to exhibit their feelings fully.

## Helping your child feel comfortable expressing their feelings and emotions

Parents need to ensure that their child feels comfortable expressing their feelings and emotions and this can be done by creating an environment where expression of feelings is encouraged. By expressing your own emotions and talking about how you are feeling, you can encourage your child to do the same. Let your child see when you are happy, praise them when they have pleased you and encourage them to talk about happy occasions and events. Likewise, if your child feels sad encourage them to share their problems and help them to work things through.

## Encouraging your child to express their feelings

Parents can encourage children to express their feelings by:

- **Respecting their child.** A child whose feelings and emotions are ridiculed is more likely to keep their feelings hidden than one whose parents accept the way they are feeling.
- **Encouraging their child to find suitable openings to vent certain feelings.** For example, an angry child can be encouraged to take part in physical play to release pent-up rage or frustration.

Although some children will find it very easy to talk about the way they are feeling, this is not the case for all of them. There are several factors which will help to determine whether a child will find it easy or difficult to talk about their emotions including:

- The response they receive from the adults around them.
- The child's own personality.
- How their parents perceive boys and girls to behave, for example some parents strongly believe that boys should not be seen to cry.
- The role models in the child's life. An open, loving and sharing family atmosphere is more likely to encourage the child to express emotion more easily.

# Shyness

Shyness can rob people of opportunities in life. Parents who recognise and address their child's shyness can help them to overcome these feelings and, hopefully, they will be less likely to carry their shyness into adulthood. There are a number of things that parents can do to help a shy child:

- Teach social skills as early as possible
- Teach your child how to tolerate and respect others
- Help your child to manage their emotions
- Encourage your child to find what they are good at and build on these talents in order to help them feel special
- Provide your child with a confident, social role model
- Encourage your child to deal with change one step at a time.

## Understanding why your child is shy

Identifying the nature of your child's shyness will help greatly when overcoming it. *When* your child is shy? Are they prone to shyness in groups of people, in public, with strangers etc.? It is important to remember that even adults who appear socially confident, who meet different people on a regular basis, or those who chair meetings and so on may still be prone to shyness. Everyone gets nervous at some time. If an adult finds mixing with new people difficult, imagine how nerve-wracking it can be for a toddler starting pre-school or a five year old going into reception class.

## Socialising before your child is ready

It is paramount that parents do not force their child to socialise before they are ready as this will damage their confidence and self-esteem and may set them back even further. Instead of forcing a child to be social, concentrate on making them feel good about themselves.

## Avoiding the 'shy' label

Many parents are guilty of labelling their children. It is never a good idea to make excuses for a child's behaviour and by telling people that your child is shy you are effectively giving them a reason to accept the way they are and avoid dealing with it. Always avoid describing a child as shy.

## Introducing your child to new people

If your child is about to start pre-school or nursery for the first time you will inevitably be worried about how they will cope. It is important to take one step at a time and to reassure your child. You need to be gentle when introducing your child to new people. Encourage them to start off slowly by saying 'hello' and praise them if they are able to complete this small task.

It is better to select a small pre-school or nursery or, if this is not possible, then try to engage your child in a small group activity within the setting. Initially it is better to get your child involved in something which interests them, rather than expecting them to choose from a huge array of new toys and equipment. Try to be as encouraging as you can and think positively. Tell yourself that your child will participate and enjoy his time at the setting in order to avoid your own apprehension rubbing off on your child.

## Is it really shyness?

Parents should be cautious when deciding whether or not they have a 'shy' child. Just because your child does not jump in to a situation with both feet does not necessarily mean that they are shy. Some children prefer to take a back seat for a little while until they have sized up a situation and this holding back should not be seen as shyness.

## Counselling

Although shyness can often be overcome, in extreme cases children may need the help of a professional. Being shy does not necessarily mean there is something wrong with your child but, it is important that any issues which result in your child being uncomfortable in social situations are addressed and often a qualified child counsellor can be useful.

# Tackling bullies

## What is bullying?

Bullying is a form of abuse which can be carried out by both adults and children. It can take on many forms, however all usually result in distress and emotional problems for the child concerned. Bullying is never a form of harmless fun. It is completely unacceptable and must be tackled immediately.

Bullying between children is common and it consists of any action which is used to hurt another child regularly and without reason. It can take the form of physical attacks, verbal abuse or emotional distress.

Ritual bullying can often take on the appearance of playful teasing and it is because bullies can be very sly and conniving that their actions are often misread or overlooked. It is paramount as a parent that you understand what constitutes bullying, that you are aware of the signs and symptoms of bullying and that you are confident when dealing with bullying issues.

Every year a number of children in the UK kill themselves due to the distress and anxiety caused through their experiences of bullying. Often in the case of bullying in schools, the teachers and governors have no idea what has been going on. However fellow students, friends and most certainly the bullies themselves are aware of the hurt and suffering being inflicted on these individuals. As a parent you may find yourself in the position of having a child who is being bullied or your own child may actually be the bully. Whichever situation you find yourself in both victims and bullies need help. Whilst no child is predestined to become a victim neither are they predestined to become a bully.

## Key components of bullying

The key components are:

- Bullying is unprovoked
- Bullying consists of physical or psychological intimidation
- Bullying occurs repeatedly over time
- Bullying creates an ongoing pattern of harassment or abuse.

## Forms of bullying

Bullying can take on many forms including:

- cruel text or email messages
- damage to property
- ignoring someone
- intimidation
- name calling
- racial insults
- rumour mongering
- sarcasm
- teasing
- theft of possessions
- threatening behaviour.

## The bully

Often people who resort to bullying do so because of their own insecurities and feelings of failure. Inflicting pain or emotional suffering on another person can often make a bully feel better about themselves. Although much of our sympathies when dealing with incidents of bullying will, quite rightly, lie with the victim, it is also the case that the bully themself needs help. In order to do this, we need to know why certain people feel they have to inflict suffering on others.

## Is your child a bully?

A child's particular temperament, the way they have been brought up by their parents and the kind of behaviour management they have experienced will all contribute to how the child feels about themself. Combine these aspects with another child who is an 'easy target', teachers who turn a blind eye or a school with a poor bullying policy and a child may begin to start showing signs of bullying behaviour.

It may be that certain traits experienced by the child in the home environment, for example aggression, increase the likelihood that a child could become a bully. This is not to say, however, that every child who experiences aggressive behaviour within the home will turn out to be a bully themselves. Sometimes children who come from homes where their parents are permissive with regard to their child's upbringing may produce children who bully.

As a parent you may find it very difficult to accept that your child is a bully. Your first reaction to your child being accused of bullying could be disbelief. It is highly likely that your child will deny that they have had anything to do with the suffering of another child and they may become defensive. It is worth bearing in mind, however, that few parents of children in school will make a complaint regarding bullying issues unless they feel they have a justified complaint. Most parents are aware of pre-school spats and childhood fall outs. It is usually when their child shows more severe signs of distress caused by persistent bullying that parents will decide to contact the school. If this is the case, denying your child's part in the bullying will be of help to no one. You need to listen to the school and talk to your child. It is important that you take what is being said seriously and work with them to find a solution. Always remember that someone's child may be going through untold misery at the hands of your own child and imagine how you would feel if the roles were reversed.

## Is my child capable of bullying?

Although most of us would find it inconceivable that our child was inflicting physical or mental torment on another, it is important to ask yourself and your child some important questions to ascertain whether or not they are capable of bullying someone.

## Finding out if your child is bullying

Ask your child if they have done any of the following to the victim they have been accused of bullying:

- Call them names
- Show any physical violence towards them including hitting, kicking, tripping them up etc.
- Damage their property
- Steal from them including taking sweets or dinner money
- Tease them even when you know they are not enjoying it
- Spread rumours or gossip about them
- Tell other people not to be their friend
- Purposely leave them out when choosing a partner or team
- Threaten them in any way
- Hide their possessions
- Make nuisance telephone calls to them or send nasty text messages
- Make racial or cultural remarks about them

- Go along with the crowd when any of the above are happening rather than be counted out.

## Bullying in a group

Bullies will sometimes work in groups and pick on individuals who are smaller or more vulnerable than themselves in order to increase their own sense of power and authority. Often the bully's peers will assume the role of perpetrator as the bully gives commands whilst looking on. It may be that your child, instead of being the actual bully, is being used as one of the bully's 'henchmen'. If this is the case, it is important that they understand that their behaviour is not acceptable and that by simply being associated with the bully and condoning their behaviour they are making someone's life a misery. It may be that your child is simply condoning the bully's behaviour because they are afraid to say no. Often children get enlisted into acting out the bully's wishes because they are afraid the tables will be turned on them if they do not.

## Why children become bullies

Bullies, like their victims, are in need of help. However, before being able to help a person who resorts to bullying we need some insight into why they are behaving in this way. Reasons for their behaviour are not *excuses* but by trying to understand what makes a bully 'tick' and taking steps to understand their behaviour it will assist parents enormously when trying to help them.

There are many reasons why some children resort to bullying such as:

- Being ignorant about what is and is not acceptable behaviour. Some children have absolutely no concept whatsoever about how they should and shouldn't behave. As a result they have no understanding of how to limit their demands or indeed why it is necessary to do so. This kind of behaviour may come about as a result of a child being denied any form of indulgence themselves by their own parents. The child has therefore come to recognise that by using threats and intimidation they are more likely to achieve what they want. At the other end of the spectrum some children, who have been spoilt and indulged excessively by their parents, may resort to bullying because the are so used to demanding their own way and have never been taught how to limit their behaviour; subsequently they expect everyone to give into their demands, resorting to harassment if necessary.

- The child may have actually been a victim of bullying themselves. Most of us would expect that a victim would be less likely to inflict the kind of pain and suffering on another person that they themselves have endured. Sadly this is not always the case and often victims will turn the tables and resort to bullying themselves. This is either because they feel it is pay back time or because they consider that by becoming the aggressor themselves they are less likely to be the victim.
- Children who have been abused in the past by adults may have difficulty understanding how to behave towards their peers and they will resort to abusive, bullying behaviour.
- Being part of a group can often trigger bullying as each member of the group competes for attention and aims to stake their position as top dog. Bullies need to be accepted by their peers and will try to impress others with their abusive behaviour. Other members of the group may be reluctant to stand up to the bully for fear of recrimination. Often group members will go along with the leader in order to remain in favour and maintain their identity within the group.
- Bullying makes people feel powerful. Often children with low self-esteem and little confidence will resort to bullying as a way of making themselves appear influential, strong and formidable.
- Sometimes a bully has an exaggerated sense of self-importance and resorts to bullying in order to reiterate these feelings.
- A fall-out amongst friends. Bullies are often former friends of their victims.
- Family problems can sometimes result in a child bullying others as they may feel insecure, unloved and full of self-doubt, and bullying others increases their sense of importance.

### Possible punishments

If your child has been found guilty of bullying at school there are several sanctions which may be applied. These may include a warning, detention, temporary or permanent exclusion from school. The age of criminal responsibility in England and Wales is ten years old and, if the bullying involves violence, text phone abuse, or demands for money, then it is possible that the victim's parents will make a complaint to the police.

## The victim

Any child can be a victim of bullying, although more often than not victims are selected because they appear outwardly different to their peers. For example, a child with red hair, or who wears glasses may be victimised by name calling as can people with differences in skin colour or an obvious disability. Children who are shy and reserved are also more likely to become victims of bullying.

Often the victim of bullying has not learned the skills associated with being able to stand up for themselves, making them an easy target. Children need to be taught how to interpret signals correctly so that they do not inadvertently mistake ambiguous signals as being threats resulting in them feeling scared and perhaps avoiding certain situations which will surely show them as being an easy target. Children need to be taught how to be assertive rather than aggressive.

### Being attentive to changes in behaviour

It can be very difficult to know when a child is being bullied unless they actually tell you, and it is therefore very important that parents are attentive to the changes in their child. Some children will try to cover up any signs of bullying for a fear of making matters worse and even if you feel you have sufficient evidence, which points to the fact that your child is being bullied, it can still be very difficult to sort things out without their co-operation.

### Why some children become victims of bullying

It is important to remember that some children inadvertently set themselves up to be victims. Children who are shy and find it difficult to make friends for example are prime targets for bullies as they can be certain that these types of children are unlikely to stand up to them or fight back. Other, more outgoing and popular, children may also become victims of bullying perhaps because of an overpowering nature or through unintentional aggravation or goading. A popular, pretty girl who appears to have lots going for her can become the victim of a jealous bully simply because she appears confident and admired; a bully may decide to take it upon themselves to bring the popular person 'down a peg or two' by subjecting them to harassment.

## Recognising bullying

If your child confides in you that they are being bullied it is essential that you act upon the revelation. Reassure your child that you believe what they are telling you and that you will do all you can to help them sort the problem out. No matter how inconsequential the bullying may appear to you, name calling can be just as traumatic to a child as a physical attack. Never dismiss the allegation or encourage your child to either keep away from their attacker or stand up to them and fight. Although parents often offer this kind of advice, particularly to sons, as they do not wish their child to appear weak or victimised, the simple truth of the matter is that this kind of advice, no matter how well meaning, will be of no benefit to the child. Faced with this kind of advice it is highly likely that the child will continue to be bullied and, worse still, will probably end up hiding the fact.

### Signs of bullying

Bullied children will often feel fearful, apprehensive, worthless, undermined and upset.

Of course, not all children will openly admit that they are being bullied and you will need to be attentive to any changes in your child if you are to help them overcome this kind of behaviour.

Some of the possible signs of bullying may include:

- Attempting to self-harm
- Bedwetting
- Being physically sick – this could be as a result of worry or may be self-inflicted to avoid having to go to school
- Complaints of illness such as tummyache and headache – children often feign illness to avoid having to go to school, or to avoid clubs or classes, if they are being bullied there
- Deterioration of school work – if the child is usually hard working and does well in class but suddenly starts to lose interest and their school work is suffering you should be concerned
- Frequently 'losing' possessions – this could be a sign of having had their possessions stolen by the bully
- Often appearing hungry – this could be a sign of having their lunch or lunch money stolen from them by the bully
- Regression – thumb sucking, rocking, comfort behaviour etc. is often a sign of uncertainty in a child who does not usually resort to this type of behaviour
- Regularly asking for, or stealing, money – this may be requested from them by the bully
- Ripped clothing – this could be a sign that the child has been involved in a fight or has been roughly handled by others
- Showing aggressive behaviour which is otherwise out of character for the child
- Suffering from troubled sleep or nightmares
- Unexplained injuries – these could be a sign of physical harm either by a bully or self-inflicted. You should be concerned if the child suddenly appears to be suffering from a lot of injuries for which they can not offer a satisfactory explanation

- Being moody and bad tempered
- Wanting to avoid leaving the house
- Falling out with previously good friends
- Being quiet and withdrawn.

## Understanding bullying

Bullying is a type of aggressive behaviour often associated with inadequacy and a need for domination. Bullies like to be in control and wield authority over their victims.

Often bullies feel unwanted or uncared for. Problems at home, such as divorce, or pressure from friends, can result in a child showing bullying tendencies.

### What to do if your child is doing the bullying

If you discover that your child is inflicting distress on another child through bullying you must act in order to sort the problem out and put an end to the victim's suffering. It is important that you do not judge your child or blame yourself for what is happening, however you need to make it clear to them that their behaviour is unacceptable and that what they are doing is hurtful, wrong and is ultimately causing another individual distress and harm.

There are a number of things you can do to try to sort the problem out:

- Talk to your child and try to get to the heart of why they feel it is necessary to behave in this way. Find out what is bothering them or triggering their behaviour
- Make sure your child understands that it is their *behaviour* you do not like rather than them
- Reassure your child that you are willing to help them and that you will work with them to find a way to change their unacceptable behaviour

- Encourage your child to make amends with their victim. Talk about how they can apologise for the suffering they have inflicted on the other person and explain why it is necessary to do so
- Offer your child lots of praise and encouragement and ensure you acknowledge when they have behaved well and managed to control their temper or feelings
- Be prepared to challenge your child if they retaliate or make excuses for their behaviour such as 'it's only a joke' or 'he's taken it all the wrong way'. Explain that jokes do not result in distress and harassment and make it clear that bullying is not funny and is never seen as harmless fun.

## Dealing with incidents of bullying

In addition to helping and understanding the behaviour of your child if they are doing the bullying, you can do a lot to help your child protect themselves against bullying.

Some of these strategies involve:

- Reassure your child that you love them and that you are on their side 100 per cent. Never dismiss your child's worries and make sure that *all* forms of bullying are treated seriously. Name calling can be just as devastating to a child as actual physical attacks and both can be extremely traumatic.
- Find out if there are any triggers which appear to start the attacks of bullying. Sometimes a child can unintentionally goad or aggravate their attacker and it is necessary to establish whether your child is unwittingly making themselves a target for the bully.
- It may be that your child is quiet and shy and therefore finds it hard to make friends. If this is the case, help them to build on their confidence and show them strategies for making friends. Encourage them to join clubs outside of school hours. There is more about shyness in Chapter 10.
- Encourage your child to be more assertive. This should not be mistaken for being aggressive. Children do not need to fight to be assertive, they simply

need to recognise that they do not have to put up with being mistreated and they should recognise that they have the right to be treated with respect.

- Reassure your child that they are not to blame for the bullying they are experiencing. Quite often both the bully and the victim will experience similar emotions of self-doubt and worthlessness.
- Try to discourage your child from crying in front of the bully or responding dramatically to their threats and behaviour. This can quite often encourage their behaviour and lead to more bullying. Insist that your child walks away and, if possible, get them to tell an adult immediately.
- Work out with your child ways of minimising opportunities for the bullying to take place. Encourage your child to spend as much time as possible around other people and to avoid spending lots of time alone.
- Encourage your child to be prepared for the bully's taunts. Quite often a child who has a planned response will feel more in control of the situation and begin to feel more assertive.
- Encourage your child to confide in a favourite teacher, someone they can talk to and feel confident about.
- Offer lots of love, praise and encouragement. A child who is being bullied will be stripped of their self-esteem and may feel useless and even deserving of the suffering they are receiving.
- It is important that adults think carefully before taking any action. Thoughtless action can be just as damaging as taking no action at all. Children need to know that the adults they confide in will see things from their perspective and understand the situation they are in.
- Wherever possible, work out a strategy *with* your child for dealing with the bullying. Do not take sudden action.

## Being strong for your child

Never let your child see how distressed the situation is making you as they may feel that you are unable to deal with it. Your child needs you to be strong and to know that you are there for them. Becoming an emotional wreck, flying off the handle or resorting to hysteria will be of little use to anyone, least of all your child. Do not be tempted to wrap your child in cotton wool or refuse to allow them to go to school. Your child's fears will escalate if they do not face them and, of course, their schooling will suffer enormously if they begin to stay away from the classroom.

Never promise to keep the information regarding bullying a secret; if you are to help your child to overcome their bullying problems then you will need to speak to their teachers, although no action should be taken without first discussing it with your child.

## Helping your child become assertive

Both bullies and their victims can benefit from learning basic self-assertive skills. Self-assertiveness can help a child to feel good about themselves and gives them a sense of well-being.

It must be understood that assertiveness is *not* the same as aggression. Most people will fall into one of three categories:

- **Passive** – These people are of the opinion that other people's rights matter more than their own. They usually lack self-esteem and confidence. Victims are often passive people.
- **Assertive** – These people respect both themselves and others equally. This is how we should strive to be.
- **Aggressive** – These people behave as if their rights are more important than the rights of others. Bullies are often aggressive people.

In order for your child to practise being assertive you will need to encourage them to:

- Avoid arguments
- Avoid getting angry and upset

- Be prepared for all eventualities – plan ahead and prepare their response
- Don't make excuses – offer alternatives
- Know their own mind and be clear about what they want
- Learn how to say 'no' and mean it. If they are not happy with a certain situation they should not be pressured into giving in but should learn to stand firm
- Learn how to 'blank' the taunts. Responding to insults with insults can end up making matters unbearable. Either ignore the insults and walk away or reply with a simple 'That's your opinion' or 'Maybe' and then walk away. If the bully doesn't get the response they are looking for, it is quite likely they will become bored and give up.

## Moving your child to another school

It is important to remember that, even with your support and the support of your child's school, the bullying may not stop immediately. By reporting an incident of bullying you are not guaranteed to get instant success and it is by no means certain that the bully will be reprimanded, learn their lesson and never resort to bullying again. Quite often putting an end to bullying is not that simple. You may find that the bully needs many reprimands, they may find the whole situation amusing or they may bully your child even more because they have had the courage to report them.

If the bullying persists then you and your child will need to continue to report the incidents so that the school can take the appropriate steps. Unless the bullying is very severe and includes incidents of violence then it is highly unlikely that the bully will be permanently excluded until all other avenues have been explored.

Moving your child to another school is not an instant solution and, although it may seem like the most obvious and relatively easy step to take this is not always the case. Firstly, you need to ask yourself why your child is being bullied. If possible address these problems as moving schools may not make any difference if they find themselves falling victim to bullying yet again in a new school.

### Considering your options

Other things you and your child will need to consider are:

- Which school will they go to next? Is there a place at this school? Is it within easy access from your home?
- How will your child feel about leaving their old friends behind?
- Will your child find it easy to make new friends, particularly if they move mid-term and are likely to be placed in a class of established friendship groups?
- Will changing schools actually put an end to the bullying or will it be possible for the bully to catch up with your child in the street or on their journey to and from school?
- How likely is it that the bully may have friends or relatives in your child's new school?

Much will depend upon the severity of the bullying your child is experiencing and how much support you have received from the school in tackling the problems. However, it is very important to consider whether or not your child will be adding to their problems rather than reducing them by moving to a different school. They may end up feeling even more isolated in a new school particularly if they find making new friends difficult.

## Bullying outside school

Although it is widely perceived that bullying of children takes place in school this is by no means the only place where your child might fall victim to bullies. If bullying takes place inside school it is easy for parents to know where to go first to seek a solution to the problem. But what happens if your child is being bullied outside the school premises, for example on the journey to and from school? Schools can take action against pupils in school uniform who carry out bullying outside the school premises, therefore if your child is experiencing problems on their journey to and from school then it is still worth contacting the head teacher and letting them know your concerns. It is highly unlikely however that a school will become involved in incidents which occur at the weekend or during school holidays.

Your child may fall victim to bullies who have no association with their school environment at all. They may find themselves being bullied by other children in the neighbourhood, for example. This kind of bullying can be very detrimental as it may result in your child not wishing to leave the house and could even result in you deciding to move house to escape the torment your child is suffering. The police are unlikely to intervene in this kind of situation although they may agree to visit the home of the bully initially to try to calm matters. However, unless there has been an actual assault with independent witnesses then no action is likely to be taken. You could try talking parent to parent with the mother or father of the bully explaining to them what is happening, though admittedly this can do more harm than good particularly if the parents of the bully deny their child's involvement.

It is always a good idea to involve your child in social activities outside of school hours where they can mix and play with other children off the streets where the bullying is a danger to them. Invite their school friends over to your house so that your child doesn't feel excluded from playing outdoors with the neighbouring children.

# Part Two

## How to Grow Healthy Kids

Part Two will help you to:

- Provide a healthy diet for your child
- Encourage your child to keep fit.

# The principles of nutrition

## Providing a healthy diet for children

The first 12 months of a child's life are very important as this is when you start building the foundations for good health. It is paramount that parents understand how to provide the proper nutrition and the correct exercise for children during their first year.

## The food pyramid

A food pyramid is an excellent way of recognising easily how much food, on average, we should be eating from each of the food groups in order to maintain a healthy balanced diet. The pyramid clearly shows that most of the food we eat should come from the breads and cereals group with the least foods falling into the fats and sugar category.

### *Daily portions from each category of the food pyramid*

Depending on age, we should be aiming to eat the following number of portions per day from each of the above categories:

- Bread, cereals and potatoes – 6 to 11 portions
- Fruit and vegetables – 5 portions
- Milk and dairy – 2 to 3 portions
- Meat, fish and pulses – 2 portions
- Fats and sweets – occasionally.

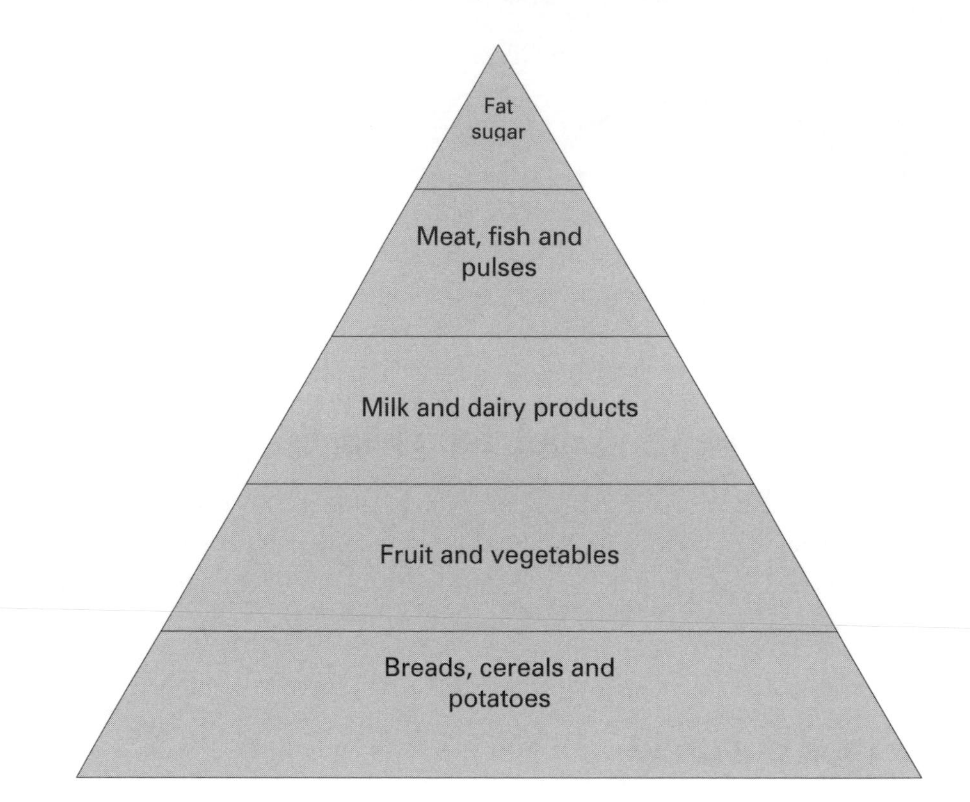


## Key nutrients

There are five different categories of nutrients and these are:

- vitamins
- protein
- carbohydrates
- minerals
- fats.

Each of these five nutrients can be divided into two groups:

- macronutrients
- micronutrients.

**Macronutrients** – these are the nutrients which we eat in large amounts (the word 'macro' means large).

**Micronutrients** – these are the nutrients which we eat in small amounts (the word 'micro' means small).

The three nutrients which fall into the group of macronutrients are:

- protein
- carbohydrates
- fat.

We need to eat relatively large quantities of these three nutrients every day in order to provide our bodies with the energy they need.

The remaining two nutrients are in the micronutrient group:

- vitamins
- minerals.

Each contains many different types of nutrient such as vitamins A, B, and C, iron, sodium and calcium. Although our bodies require all of these nutrients in order to remain healthy we only need to consume small amounts of each.

# Macronutrients

## Carbohydrates

Carbohydrates can be split into two different forms:

- simple carbohydrates
- complex carbohydrates.

### *Simple carbohydrates*

These take very little time to be converted into energy and can be found mainly in the following foods:

- sugar
- fruit
- fizzy drinks
- biscuits
- cakes and chocolate
- jam and honey.

### *Complex carbohydrates*

These take longer to be converted into energy and can be found in the following foods:

- pasta
- bread
- potatoes
- rice
- breakfast cereals.

The main function of carbohydrates is to supply the body with energy. We need energy to take part in any form of physical activity, and the more physical activity we take part in the more carbohydrates we will need to consume. A lack of carbohydrates would leave us feeling tired and lethargic. The brain needs a constant supply of carbohydrates in order to function adequately and a diet which does not contain sufficient carbohydrates could lead to a lack of concentration and energy.

## Protein

Protein is essential in our diet in order for the body to grow and repair itself. Many parts of our body are made up of protein including muscles, skin, hair, nails and internal organs. Protein can be found in many of the foods we eat which are derived both from animals or animal products such as:

- meat
- fish
- poultry
- eggs
- milk and milk products
- nuts
- beans.

A lack of protein in the body may lead to hair loss, muscle weakening or wasting and delayed healing of wounds.

## Fats

Fat provides the body with energy; it has twice as many calories per gram as carbohydrates and protein although the energy produced from fat is supplied at a very slow rate. Fat is therefore used for activities which are less energetic such as walking and sitting. Fat also provides the body with insulation which ensures that the body remains at a certain temperature and does not get too cold. Another important job of the fat in the body is to protect our internal organs by acting as a shock absorber should we fall or hit ourselves hard. A lack of fat in the diet may lead to dry and flaky skin.

Fat can be found in food products such as:

- meat
- cheese

- cream and milk
- butter and margarine
- lard
- chocolate
- cooking oil
- oily fish such as sardines
- nuts and seeds.

A lack of fat in the diet is very rare in the western world – most people are actually eating too much fat in their diet which leads to other health problems such as obesity and heart disease.

# Micronutrients

## Vitamins

Vitamins can be divided into two main groups:

- Fat soluble, which can be stored in the body until needed
- Water soluble, which cannot be stored and which are excreted if we consume more than we need.

Our bodies are unable to make vitamins and it is therefore essential that we eat a diet which will provide us with the right amount of vitamins. Most of the food we consume contains some form of vitamin, however in order to ensure that we receive sufficient quantities of each it is essential that we eat a varied, balanced diet.

## Essential vitamins

Essential vitamins needed by the body are A, B, C, D and E.

### *Vitamin A*

This ensures that we maintain good vision, skin and hair. A lack of vitamin A in the diet could lead to night-blindness. Vitamin A can be found in the following foods:

- dark green vegetables
- liver
- carrots
- beef
- mackerel.

Vitamin A comes in two forms:

1. Preformed Vitamin A – known as retinol – which is only found in foods of animal origin and
2. Provitamin A – known as carotene – which is found in food of both plant and animal origin.

Vitamin A is often shown on commercial food labels as the additive *beta carotene* and this is the preferred form for supplementation.

### *Vitamin B*

This helps our bodies to break down the food which we eat in order to provide us with energy. Vitamin B also helps with blood production and promotes normal appetite. A lack of vitamin B in the diet could lead to anaemia. Vitamin B can be found in the following foods:

- liver
- eggs
- beef and pork

- beans
- cereals.

### Vitamin C

This helps us to fight infection and maintain healthy skin and gums. Vitamin C also aids healing. A lack of vitamin C in the diet could lead to bleeding gums and the slow healing of wounds. Vitamin C can be found in the following foods:

- fresh fruit, particularly citrus fruits such as oranges and lemons
- fresh vegetables
- potatoes.

### Vitamin D

This helps our bodies to develop strong teeth and bones. A lack of vitamin D in the diet could lead to rickets. Vitamin D can be found in sunlight and the following foods:

- eggs
- oily fish
- milk
- dairy products.

### Vitamin E

This helps us to maintain healthy body cells and protect them from damage it also provides the body with more energy thus alleviating fatigue. A lack of vitamin E in the diet could lead to anaemia and eye damage. Vitamin E can be found in the following foods:

- nuts
- margarine
- dark green leafy vegetables such as cabbage and spinach
- whole grains.

## Minerals

In order for us to maintain a healthy body it is vital that we eat a huge range of minerals including calcium, iron, iodine, sulfur, potassium, manganese, sodium and cobalt. We can ensure we consume all of these minerals by eating a balance and varied diet. However the three main minerals required by the body are:

- calcium
- iron
- iodine.

### *Calcium*

This helps to build strong bones and teeth and enables the body to form blood clots. A lack of calcium in the diet may lead to rickets or osteoporosis. Calcium can be found in the following foods:

- milk
- fish bones such as pilchards and sardines
- leafy green vegetables such as cabbage.

### *Iron*

This helps with the production of blood. A lack of iron in the diet may lead to anaemia. Iron can be found in the following foods:

- lean meat
- liver
- eggs
- dried fruit.

### *Iodine*

This is essential for our bodies to control the rate at which we break down and use the nutrients we consume. A lack of iodine in the diet may lead to lethargy, skin problems and low energy levels. Iodine can be found in the following foods:

- fish
- sea food.

## Non-nutrients

We now know that the body requires nutrients which provide the body with energy and which help us to grow. It is also important to remember that we need to consume some foods and drinks which, although they do not provide us with any energy or help us to grow, are still necessary in order for our bodies to function properly. These foods are known as 'non-nutrient foods'.

Non-nutrient foods fall into four main categories:

- water
- fibre
- alcohol
- flavours and colours.

Of these four categories only water and fibre are essential for the human body to function properly.

## Water

We all know how important water is. Although we could survive for many days without food it is highly unlikely that we would survive for more than three days without water. The main functions of water are to:

- transport important nutrients around the body
- control body temperature through the process of sweating
- enable us to rid the body of waste products through the process of urination and defecation.

We can consume an adequate amount of water by drinking pure water, drinking fruit juice/tea/coffee and other beverages and by eating foods which have a high water content.

## Fibre

Fibre helps to move food through the digestive system. Fibre is essential in order to maintain a smooth passage of faeces through the body and avoid constipation. Fibre absorbs water into our faecal matter making it softer and bulkier which in turn enables the digestive process to run smoothly. Fibre can be found in grains, wholemeal bread, pasta and brown rice.

## Alcohol

Many teenagers experiment with alcohol and it is necessary to be aware of how it affects the body. Alcohol is a toxin and acts as a depressant; it contains high quantities of sugar and is absorbed into the blood stream from the stomach and small intestine and then carried around the body: it is carried to the brain through the blood. Too much alcohol can impair judgement and affect co-ordination.

## Flavours and colours

Most foods have colour and flavour added to them to make them look and taste better. All food colourings and flavourings have to go through an approval process in order to ensure that they are safe to use in the European Union and they will carry a letter 'E' along with a number. Although approved, many 'E' numbers have been linked to various problems in children such as hyperactivity and asthma.

In theory additives are supposed to be safe. However they can provoke allergic reactions in some children. Foods which contain the highest amounts of additives are sweets, savoury snacks, desserts and snack bars. Some of the most common additives in food which you should look out for on labels are:

| | |
|---|---|
| **Colourings**: | Tartrazine (E102) |
| | Sunset Yellow (E110) |
| | Carmoisine (E122) |
| | Ponceau 4R (E124) |
| **Preservatives**: | Sodium Benzoate (E211) |

## Encouraging healthy eating and food choices

Below are some practical tips for encouraging healthy eating and food choices as outlined by the Food Standards Agency:

- Base meals on starchy foods.
- Eat lots of fruit and vegetables.
- Eat more fish.
- Cut down on saturated fat and sugar.
- Eat less salt.
- Get active.
- Drink plenty of water.
- Don't skip breakfast.

Let us now look at these eight tips in more detail:

## Base meals on starchy food

Starchy foods consist of items such as:

- ✓ bread
- ✓ cereals
- ✓ pasta
- ✓ rice
- ✓ potatoes.

Starchy foods should make up approximately a third of the food we eat. Starchy foods are a good source of energy; in addition to containing starch these foods also contain fibre, calcium, iron and B vitamins. We should be aiming to include at least one of these starchy foods in each of our meals. Although many people avoid starchy foods because they consider them to be fattening they actually contain less than half the calories of fat gram for gram. Calorie content usually increases with the fats added when cooking and serving these particular foods.

When choosing starchy foods, opt for wholegrain, whenever possible. Wholegrain foods contain more fibre and other nutrients than white starchy foods. Wholegrain foods are also digested more slowly and therefore help us to feel full for longer. Wholegrain foods include:

- wholemeal and wholegrain bread
- pitta
- chapatti
- wholewheat pasta
- brown rice
- wholegrain breakfast cereal.

## Eat lots of fruit and vegetables

It is common knowledge that we need to eat lots of fruit and vegetables and most people are aware of their importance, however most of us still aren't consuming an adequate amount on a daily basis. We should be aiming to eat a minimum of five portions a day, and these could be in the form of:

- a piece of fruit as a snack
- slices of fruit added to breakfast cereal
- a glass of fruit juice
- a side salad
- a portion of vegetables with your evening meal.

Fruit and vegetables can take the form of fresh, frozen, tinned, dried or juices. It is important to remember that potatoes, although a vegetable, are classed as a starchy food and not as a portion of fruit and vegetables.

## Eat more fish

Fish is an excellent source of protein and most of us should be eating more – at least one portion of oily fish per week. Oily fish is particularly beneficial as it is rich in certain types of fats known as omega 3 fatty acids which can help to keep the heart healthy. Examples of oily fish are salmon, mackerel, trout, herring, sardines, pilchards and fresh tuna. Examples of non-oily fish which are also healthy food choices are cod, haddock, plaice, coley, skate, hake and tinned tuna. Some fish contain high levels of mercury and should not be consumed more than once a week, these include swordfish, marlin and shark. Although fish may be fresh, frozen or canned it is important to bear in mind that canned and smoked fish may be high in salt.

## Cut down on saturated fat and sugar

There are two main types of fat: saturated and unsaturated. Saturated fat can increase the amount of cholesterol in the blood which increases the chance of developing heart disease if too much is eaten. Unsaturated fat lowers blood cholesterol and is essential for remaining healthy. We should aim to cut down on foods which are high in saturated fat such as meat pies, sausages, hard cheese, butter, lard, pastry, cakes, biscuits and cream, and eat foods which are rich in unsaturated fat such as vegetable oils, oily fish, avocados, nuts and seeds.

Most people in the United Kingdom eat too much sugar. We should always be striving to eat fewer foods which contain added sugar such as sweets, cakes, biscuits and fizzy drinks. Foods which are high in sugar increase the chance of tooth decay and are high in calories. Sugar is often described on food labels as sucrose, glucose, fructose, maltose, corn syrup and honey. If one of these descriptions features near the top of the ingredients list it is an indication that the food is high in added sugar.

## Eat less salt

Even if you don't actually add salt to your meals this can not guarantee that your salt intake is not too high. Adults and children over the age of 11 should not be consuming more than 6g of salt per day – children under the age of 11 should be having even less. 75 per cent of the salt we eat is already in the food that we buy, such as breakfast cereals, ready-made meals, soups and sauces, therefore you may be getting more salt than is recommended without actually realising it. Eating too much salt can raise your blood pressure and people with high blood pressure are three times more likely to develop heart disease or have a stroke.

## Get active

Ideally you should be neither overweight nor underweight as both can affect your health. Physical activity is an excellent way of using up extra calories and helps to control weight. Try to be active every day and build up the amount of daily exercise you take. Walking as much as possible at a good pace will help you to start getting active.

## Drink plenty of water

We should be aiming to drink between six and eight glasses of water, or other fluids, every day in order to combat dehydration. When the weather is warm or after any kind of physical activity we should increase our fluid intake but avoid soft and fizzy drinks which are high in added sugar.

## Don't skip breakfast

Breakfast is one of the most important meals as it sets us up for the day and provides us with essential energy. Missing meals is not a good way of controlling calorie intake as we also miss out on essential nutrients.

# The principles of fitness

## Getting children physically fit

Unfortunately not all children are natural athletes and sometimes it is a battle of wills to get children into regular physical exercise. The trick here is to build on their interests and to make exercise *fun*. If a child sees exercising as a chore they are more likely to refuse to join in and demand the television be switched on. However, think about how young children enjoy a game of 'chase' or squeal with delight when kicking a football – exercise can and should be fun! Taking the dog for a walk can be less boring if you take along a selection of balls to throw for Fido or play a game of hide and seek in the woods – incorporating imaginative games into exercise ensures it is fun, versatile and enjoyable.

## Avoiding 'couch potatoes'

Encouraging children to eat a sensible healthy diet, although good, is not the complete answer to ensuring that they lead a healthy lifestyle.

Many children used to walk to and from school every day in all weathers which was a good form of exercise now, however, the majority of children travel to school either by car or bus eliminating the exercise everyone previously took for granted. Outdoor play for children has also decreased significantly over the years with parents preventing their children from playing on the streets or in local parks for fear of abduction, robbery or other unwanted attention and now a large proportion of our young people spend their evenings, weekends and school holidays in front of the television, play station or other computer controlled entertainment, none of which benefit them physically.

Exercise in the early years needs to be fun and enjoyable if we are to set a precedent for our children to enjoy a continuous healthy lifestyle. Children need space to run, stretch and explore and, whilst space can sometimes be limited indoors, gardens, parks, playgrounds and so on provide excellent opportunities for children to exercise outside. Outdoor play and exercise should be encouraged all year round and can be enjoyed whatever the weather.

## Benefits of physical exercise

Physical exercise benefits children in a number of ways:

- It improves balance
- It improves co-ordination
- It improves flexibility
- It strengthens muscles
- It strengthens joints
- It improves appetite
- It increases bone density
- It increases blood circulation
- It develops strength and stamina
- It develops lung capacity
- It helps the digestive process.

All of these give the child a feeling of well being, and physical exercise also encourages interaction and cooperation.

When we talk about physical development we automatically think of exercise and outdoor play but physical exercise covers much more than just gross motor skills.

## Motor skills, co-ordination and balance

Physical development covers the whole body and exercise is about how children learn to control every part of their body including:

- **Gross motor skills** – movements which involve the arms and legs such as throwing and kicking a ball.
- **Fine motor skills** – small movements involving the whole of the hand such as catching a ball. Fine manipulative skills may also fall into this category such as controlling a pencil when learning to write or draw.
- **Co-ordination skills** – the ability to combine two or more skills at the same time. Co-ordinating the eye and foot for example whilst negotiating stairs or using the hand and eye when building bricks or threading beads.
- **Balance** – Closely linked with co-ordination. Children learn how to control their bodies whilst riding a bike for example, or walking in a straight line.
- **Locomotive skills** – these skills involve controlling how the child runs, jumps and walks.

### *Pacing*

Expecting too much from your child initially when exercising or pushing them too far too soon may risk putting them off completely and could potentially damage their opinion of exercise in the long term. Allow the children to explore at their own pace and to do only what they are happy and confident doing. Avoid over encouragement and never goad them into trying something they are not ready for as, in addition to this being dangerous, they may also lose confidence if they are unable to carry out a certain task.

## Ways to get children active

The most vigorous activities will probably take place outdoors. However it is important that we encourage both gross and fine motor skills indoors as well as out. It should be relatively easy for most people to be able to incorporate indoor physical play.

Dance, drama, active games, action rhymes and indoor obstacle courses are excellent ways of helping children to develop an awareness of how their bodies work whilst making the process fun and enjoyable.

## Dance

Most children enjoy dancing and this can be done either through listening to music and moving freely or by building up set dance steps and routines which the children can learn. Encourage your child to select their own music and allow them to have a say in how the dance routine takes shape.

## Drama

Drama can be used to extend other learning opportunities and most children will enjoy acting out their favourite story. Older children can use drama as an extension of a theme for example learning about Easter could be developed into a play and extended to incorporate an Easter egg hunt.

## Action rhymes

Action rhymes can be enjoyed from a very young age and most children will quickly learn the actions to repetitive rhymes such as 'Old McDonald Had a Farm'. Actions can be extended or simplified depending on the age and understanding of the child. Songs with actions are a very enjoyable way of incorporating exercise. Some examples are:

- 'Ring a Ring o'Roses'
- 'The Farmer's in his Den'
- 'The Grand Old Duke of York'
- 'If You're Happy and You Know It (stamp your feet, clap your hands etc.)'

- 'The Okey Cokey'
- 'Oranges and Lemons'
- 'Row, Row, Row your Boat'.

## Active games

Active games are another great way of encouraging children to participate in indoor exercise. Consider introducing games such as:

- Simon Says
- Musical Chairs
- Musical Statues
- Follow My Leader
- Blind Man's Bluff.

Games such as Twister and Globe Trotting arc fun to play and encourage exercise. These types of games require the child to stretch in order to place certain parts of their bodies on certain areas of a mat according to the instructions on the dial. For example Globe Trotting may require the participant to place their right hand on Europe whilst their left leg may be in North America!

## Indoor obstacle course

This can be very similar to an outdoor obstacle course but you could substitute footballs for soft foam balls or bean bags to avoid damage to furniture and furnishings.

It is possible to purchase various resources such as crazy golf and skittles which can be used just as effectively indoors as out. These resources are usually made of soft materials which are ideal for indoor use.

## Outdoor exercise

It is perhaps much easier to think of ways for children to take part in physical exercise outdoors as space is not limited. There are many different games that children can take part in such as traditional ball games like:

- football
- cricket
- rugby
- tennis
- golf.

Other team games, such as Tug of War are ideal for outdoor play. The games can be simplified for young children by allowing them to kick, throw and hit a ball.

## Outdoor obstacle course

An outdoor obstacle course using hoops, balls, cones, skittles, skipping ropes and bean bags is an excellent way of exercising and this will encourage a variety of skills including balance and co-ordination. The course can be altered and extended as the child progresses.

## Ride-on toys

Ride-on toys, bicycles, tricycles, toy cars and other vehicles are another good source of exercise and strengthen the legs and improve balance. Fix stabilisers to bicycles initially and remove them once the child has gained sufficient balance.

## Sand and water

Sand and water play is probably better suited for outdoors due to the amount of mess it can inevitably create. Children love to experiment with sand and water and this is an excellent way of improving fine motor skills by building sandcastles, sieving the sand, mixing sand with water and so on.

### Alternative outdoor areas

Not all outdoor activity needs to take place in the garden – you may not actually have a garden or outdoor area for the children to enjoy. If this is the case then consider other ways in which children can enjoy outdoor play and exercise. You can incorporate visits to the local playground or park into your routine to ensure children get regular opportunities for outdoor play and exercise. Although walking is a good source of exercise, children need the chance to run around and explore open areas such as parks and playgrounds as well.

## Staying fit for life

Most children begin their life fit, healthy and active. Think of the boundless energy of the average three or four year old and how they seem to run everywhere, jump climb and generally have difficulty sitting still! Compare this with the average teenager who spends hours in front of the television or refuses to get out of bed before lunchtime on a weekend, and you may begin to wonder where it all went wrong.

### Obstacles to exercise

Just as our own lives change, with ever-increasing demands on our time, so too do our children's. Children often encounter barriers to exercise as they get older and sometimes the desire to remain physically fit is overtaken by the need to do other things such as:

- **Homework** – often the amount of homework increases as a child gets older and, when important exams are looming, the need to study takes priority.
- **Inaccessibility of clubs** – not all children have access to local sports clubs and swimming pools and sometimes the distance to travel can be an obstacle.

- **Safety** – concerns about safety often prevent children from having the freedom to roam their own neighbourhoods.
- **Expense** – some sports can be expensive and if special equipment and clothing are needed in addition to the cost of joining clubs this can put an extra burden on parents.
- **Lack of parent's time** – just as children may have added demands on their time so too do their parents. Long working hours can make it difficult for parents to find the time to ferry children to and from clubs or give them encouragement and supervision.

### *Solutions to the problems*

- **Homework** – plan a suitable rota with your child to ensure that they have at least one evening per week free of study or make time at the weekend where your child can have a set amount of hours away from their text books.
- **Inaccessibility of clubs** – talk to local schools or contact your local authority for details of sporting events in your area. Remember it is not necessary to have a state-of-the-art sports centre in your village or town in order to access physical exercise.
- **Safety** – teach children the importance of safe play. Set guidelines with time limits for them to be away from home and make sure that you know exactly where they are at all times. Always make sure that they do not go out alone. If possible, arrange to take it in turns with other parents to stage exercise events in the garden or supervise exercise in the local park or playground on a rota basis.
- **Expense** – it is important to remember that exercise does not need to be expensive. It is not necessary to pay extortionate gym fees in order for your children to lead a healthy lifestyle. Footballs, skipping ropes, frisbees and hoops are inexpensive fun ways to keep fit! If your child does show an interest in a particular sport which may prove expensive to kit out, talk to other parents and see if you can buy the clothing their children have grown out of. Many clubs offer this service – look on the notice board or read the newsletters.

- **Lack of parent's time** – as previously mentioned talk to the parents of your children's friends and organise a rota with them so that you take it in turns to transport the children to sports clubs or the swimming baths. An hour's supervision once a week is in most parents' grasp even if they can't commit the time on a daily basis.

# Meal planning

## Breakfast – the right start to the day

Breakfast is *the* most important meal of the day. It gives children the energy they need and makes them better able to concentrate. It is therefore essential that children are encouraged to eat a *healthy* breakfast. Throwing a bag of crisps or a chocolate bar at them at 7am is not healthy!

Parents lead busier lives now than ever before and you may be tempted, at times, to ignore the importance of a good breakfast and forfeit the time it takes to prepare in favour of an extra ten minutes in bed. Tempting though this may be it is important to get into a regular routine to avoid your children getting into the habit of skipping breakfast regularly.

### What should I prepare for my child's breakfast?

Preparing a healthy breakfast need not be a time-consuming task and even a light breakfast is better than no breakfast at all.

Breakfast can be either a light meal or something more substantial. This will depend on your child and their personal appetite and needs. Never give a child too much. A large breakfast presented to a child with a small appetite will not encourage them to eat and could even end up with them refusing breakfast altogether.

Take your cue from your child when it comes to preparing a healthy breakfast and build on the foods they already like and enjoy.

### *Suitable breakfast foods*

- **Cereal** – probably the most obvious breakfast food. It is important to take care when choosing which breakfast cereals to buy as many are high in salt and sugar. Fortified breakfast cereals, which are low in salt and sugar, are an excellent way of starting the day and are also good for serving as quick snacks throughout the day. Fortified cereals provide a wealth of vitamins including folic acid, iron and zinc.
- **Porridge** – an excellent cereal which provides fibre and reduces cholesterol.
- **Wholemeal toast** – if your child prefers toast rather than cereal give them wholemeal toast which is good for the digestive tract.
- **Milk** – provides essential vitamins and minerals.
- **Yoghurt** – contains calcium and essential B vitamins.
- **Fruit** – provides essential vitamins and minerals. A piece of fruit for breakfast counts towards the all-important five-a-day fruit and vegetable consumption (there is more about five-a-day in Chapter 29).
- **Fruit juice** – like whole pieces of fruit, juice also provides essential vitamins and mineral and counts towards their five-a-day intake.
- **Eggs** – are a good source of protein and are rich in vitamin A.

## Sit down to eat

Although it may not be possible for the whole family to sit down to breakfast together it is still important for you to encourage your children to sit down at the table to eat. Setting breakfast out at the table not only makes the meal more civilised, it encourages a relaxed meal time without distractions.

Sitting down with your children at breakfast lets them see that you consider this meal to be important. It gives them a positive role model and hopefully will encourage them to look forward to the meal which starts the day off on the right foot.

### Portion sizes

Although it is important to make sure that your child has sufficient food at meal times, to ensure that they are full and will not resort to snacking on unhealthy foods between meals, such as crisps, biscuits and sweets, it is also important to check carefully the portion sizes you offer. Too small a portion will not provide your child with the sustenance they need and snacking will be inevitable. Offering too large a portion may result in them struggling, or eating more food than their body actually needs leading to obesity and an unhealthy attitude towards food.

## Shopping for the right foods

Shopping for food with children can be a nightmare. Manufacturers know that children are attracted to bright, fun packaging and that they are easily swayed by promotions. Unfortunately, it is often the case that the products aimed at children in this kind of attractive packaging is loaded with sugar, fat, salt and artificial additives.

It is therefore *very* important that you set some ground rules when supermarket shopping with children and, if you have to take your children along with you, lay down some terms and do not allow your children to sway your judgement.

Don't allow your children to pester you to buy foods which you know to be unhealthy. Your children may try to wear you down and, to avoid a confrontation in public, you may be tempted to give in, however if you give in once you will undermine your own authority for future supermarket visits and your children will try to win you over on every occasion. Make a shopping list of the things you need and *stick to it.*

Some important tips to remember when supermarket shopping with children:

- Resist shopping for food when either you or the children are hungry or tired. At these times your resistance will be low and it will be much easier for your children to win you over and persuade you to buy unhealthy food.
- Make a list and only buy the things on it.

- Avoid temptation by skipping the aisles in the supermarket which you know stock crisps, sweets, cakes, biscuits and fizzy drinks. If your children don't see the products they are less likely to pester you for them!

## The importance of checking food labels

Food labels contain an enormous amount of helpful information, providing we know what to look for and how to use the information we are given. Most packaged food provides customers with information about the food contained within. Pre-packed food will usually have a label which states:

- The cost per kg of food
- The actual cost of the particular item
- The weight of the food
- A description of the variety in the case of fruit or vegetables
- A description of the cut in the case of meat
- The country where the food was produced
- Details of whether the food is organic
- Ingredients in the food (including any which have been added)
- Nutritional composition of the food.

## High, medium and low fat, sugar and salt content

At the start of 2007 it was made a requirement for all food labels on packaged, processed foods to contain nutritional information relating to the amount of each of the following contained within the food:

- salt content
- sugar content

- saturates (including saturated fat)
- energy content.

In order to make it easier for the consumer to understand the information provided on food packages the government, through the Food Standards Agency, has begun promoting a special system which highlights the levels of each of the four components listed above contained in 100g of food. This system is known as the 'traffic light' system.

- **GREEN** – this indicates *low* amounts per 100g of food
- **AMBER** – this indicates *medium* amounts per 100g of food
- **RED** – this indicates *high* amounts per 100g of food

By recognising and understanding this traffic light system consumers should be able to tell at a glance whether the food they are choosing is healthy or unhealthy. Food labels which show **green** indicators point to the food being healthy whereas food labels which show **amber** and **red** indicators are less good for our health.

Claims on food labels can often be misleading such as yoghurt which may be advertised as being 'low fat'. Many consumers will take this to mean that they are low in *calories,* which is simply not the case. Many yoghurts actually contain high levels of sugar and are therefore high in calories. Another advertising ploy is to label food with the words 'diet' leading many to believe that the product is healthy because it contains no sugar when in actual fact the natural sugar has simply been replaced with artificial sweeteners. Always pay special attention to food labels which state that the product is 'healthy' as quite often these foods can still contain high levels of unhealthy substances such as fat, sugar and salt.

Although the traffic light system is simple to use and is, in many cases, recommended by doctors and health charities, many food manufacturers chose not to use this system and opt instead for providing information on food labels which give the proportion of 'Guideline Daily Amounts' (GDA) which each food provides. Providing GDA makes it harder for consumers to see at a glance what the food contains and they need to take the time to read the label more closely and, in many cases, shoppers do not understand the information and rely mainly on their own judgement rather than factual information to decide whether the product is nutritional or not.

## Pleasing everyone

I am not going to pretend that it is easy to plan meals which are nutritionally balanced, healthy and which *please everyone*. This is not an easy task quite simply because every member of your household will have their own preferences and, unless you are very lucky, these preferences will differ considerably. You may have a child who loves vegetables but hates meat and another who will happily devour carrots but won't touch anything green!

You will need to use your knowledge of your own children together with your persuasive techniques to get them to eat what you put in front of them! Telling your child that the meal is healthy and therefore 'good for them' is highly unlikely to do the trick and often this kind of statement is like a red rag to a bull – it seems to be a fundamental fact that all children are allergic to healthy foods!

Most children will, at some point in their lives, become 'fussy eaters'. It can be very frustrating for parents when trying to feed children who refuse to eat proper meals and the trick here is perseverance. Children will not voluntarily starve themselves and if they are holding out on eating a healthy meal with the hope that you will relent and allow them to binge on sweets and crisps then you may have to be prepared for a battle of wills which, inevitably, you *need* to win if you are to avoid a lengthy confrontation at every meal time.

### Tips to avoid meal-time confrontations

- Provide your child with a healthy balanced meal. If they refuse to eat it make sure they remain at the table until everyone else has finished their meal.
- Do not offer alternatives – if your child is hungry they will ensure they eat enough to provide for their needs.

- Do not give them any attention for refusing to eat – this is often what they are looking for.
- Praise them if they eat some of the food.

Trying to please everyone, though difficult, is not impossible. Build on the food stuffs you know your family like and think of ways to incorporate these ingredients into more imaginative meals. Dull, boring meals can be an instant turn off so try using healthy ingredients to produce tasty dishes which all the family will enjoy.

# Safety in the kitchen

## Ensuring your kitchen is hygienic

It is essential that you are aware of how to cook and store food correctly so that there is no danger of food poisoning to your child. Babies and young children are particularly prone to food poisoning and a high standard of personal hygiene must be practised at all times in order to eliminate any risk. Always remember that, as a parent, you are your child's first teacher and the practices you follow will inevitably be copied by your child.

### Basic hygiene in the kitchen

By following some simple rules for hygiene in the kitchen you can avoid the risk of contamination and the spread of infection. Always:

- Dispose of waste food carefully.
- Clean up any spills immediately using a suitable anti-bacterial solution.
- Ensure that pets are not allowed on work surfaces and that their feeding bowls are washed and stored separately.
- Wipe down work surfaces, cookers, hobs, microwaves etc. with a suitable anti-bacterial solution.

## Food safety

You need to ensure that the food you purchase is of good quality and that it is handled, stored, prepared and cooked appropriately. Babies and young children are particularly susceptible to illnesses derived from poorly prepared or cooked food and, if infected, they can become seriously ill.

When you are shopping for food stick to these important rules:

- Always check food for the 'sell by', 'best before' (best before the date but can still be consumed safely) or 'use by' (use by the date or throw away) dates. Never buy inferior quality foods which have surpassed these dates. If you have already purchased food and not consumed it within these dates then it is better to throw it away than risk infection.
- Never buy cans which are dented or swollen.
- Never buy food which has soiled packaging.
- Never buy food which has leaked from the packaging.
- Never buy food whose packaging appears to have been tampered with as this may indicate that the goods have been re-packaged to avoid 'sell by', 'best before' or 'use by' dates.
- If frozen food is not solid to the touch do not buy it.
- If the packaging on frozen food is soiled do not buy it as this may indicate that the food has thawed out and been re-frozen.
- Check the 'load line' and temperature of fridges and freezers in store. If they do not appear cold enough or if food is stacked above the 'load line' do not purchase food from them.
- Make sure that you purchase frozen or refrigerated foods last and take them home immediately. Never leave them in your car to get warm whilst shopping for other items and, if possible, try to arrange for delivery from the store directly to your house as the food is kept frozen and refrigerated en route.
- Whenever possible buy fresh food.

## Storing food

It is absolutely essential that you are aware of how to store and prepare food safely if you are to avoid contamination and infection. You can ensure safety by following these simple rules:

- Make sure that your refrigerator is set no higher than 5°C – use a thermometer if you are unsure.
- Make sure that your freezer is set at 18°C.
- Always cover any food which is left out to avoid the spread of bacteria and eliminate the risk from flies etc.
- Never re-freeze food which has been allowed to thaw out.
- Never overfill your refrigerator – air must be able to circulate round the refrigerator in order for the correct temperature to be maintained.
- Once you have opened a can of food or fruit juice transfer any leftovers to a leak-proof container before storing in the refrigerator. It is worth remembering that once a can has been opened and air has been introduced the contents can be affected.
- Cans, dried foods and packets should be stored in a cool dry place.
- Always take note of the 'sell by', 'use by' and 'best before' dates. Often people think that canned food has an unlimited shelf life – this is not true and the contents of cans should be consumed within twelve months of purchase or before the expiry date on the label otherwise they should be thrown away.
- Soft fruit, vegetables and salads should be stored in the refrigerator. If you have to leave fruit in a fruit bowl or vegetables in a rack make sure these cannot become contaminated by flies or animals.
- Take care when storing food in the refrigerator. Remember raw meats can drip blood and juices – which invariably contain harmful bacteria – onto other foods and so must never be stored on the top shelves. Always place

food items which can leak in a suitable container and store in the bottom of the refrigerator.

- Never store raw and cooked foods next to one another.

## Preparing food

Children love to help to prepare meals and snacks and baking sessions are an excellent learning opportunity for children. However, if you and your child do not stick to safe practices when preparing food, then the result could be food poisoning! Use your baking sessions to teach children the importance of handling, storing and preparing food correctly so that they will learn these important points along with learning how to cook.

Let your child see you wash your hands thoroughly before handling or eating food and encourage them to do the same – remember it takes no less than 30 seconds to wash hands effectively.

Always make sure you:

- Use different boards to chop vegetables, slice bread and cut raw meat as the blood and juices from raw meat can contaminate other foods. Plastic chopping boards are the easiest to keep clean and the most hygienic.
- Use different plates, knives and utensils for different foods.
- Allow food to thaw out in the refrigerator in a leak-proof container rather than on the kitchen work surface where bacteria can quickly multiply.
- Allow food to thaw thoroughly before cooking.
- Always ensure that you follow the manufacturer's cooking instructions which can be found on the food label when storing, heating or cooking food.

Remember that boiling point is 100°C and harmful bacteria in food is not destroyed until food has been cooked to a temperature of 71°C; it is absolutely essential that food is cooked thoroughly, at the correct temperature and for the correct length of time, to avoid food poisoning.

## Cooking food

There are several main ways in which foods can be cooked and these are shown in the table below:

| Ways of cooking food | What happens to the food when cooked in this way |
|---|---|
| Boiling in water | Vitamins B and C dissolve in the cooking water |
| Steaming | Cooks food gently with less vitamin loss |
| Baking | Food takes longer to cook in a dry oven and Vitamin B and C are destroyed |
| Grilling | Uses radiant heat to cook making the surface of the food hotter than the middle. Care needs to be taken to ensure that food is cooked thoroughly. |
| Frying | Calorie content increases as the food soaks up the hot oil or fat used to fry it |
| Microwaving | Cooks food quickly with less vitamin loss |

## Food poisoning

There are 70–80,000 food poisoning cases reported in the UK every year and potentially millions of other cases which go unrecognised. Sticking to some simple rules of hygiene in the kitchen can help you to avoid these dangers.

Food poisoning occurs when people eat food that has been contaminated with harmful micro-organisms (bacteria and viruses) or with harmful substances (toxins deriving from micro-organisms, plants, fish, chemicals and metals). Many bacteria are dangerous to humans such as those associated with food poisoning. However it is important to remember that not *all* bacteria are harmful.

Bacteria enters the body through the digestive system and as such symptoms of food poisoning will generally be in this part of the body for example, nausea, vomiting, stomach pain/cramps and diarrhoea. Food poisoning usually lasts for a couple of days and in very severe cases can lead to serious illness or even death.

Bacteria needs four key elements to grow:

- food
- warmth
- moisture
- time.

Bacteria reproduces by multiplication therefore one bacterium initially becomes two and then two become four, four become eight and so on. In the right conditions it is easy to see how one bacterium can become several millions in a relatively short space of time. Leaving food overnight on a kitchen work surface will put it at severe risk of becoming contaminated by morning.

Although placing food in a refrigerator will not completely eliminate the chance of bacteria taking shape it will slow down the multiplication of bacteria by preventing the food from becoming warm. Placing contaminated food in a refrigerator will, however, increase the spread of bacteria through cross contamination. Cross contamination is most likely to happen when raw food touches or drips onto ready-to-eat food, equipment or surfaces or when someone touches raw food and then ready-to-eat food without first washing their hands. Raw meat, if stored carelessly, may drip juices onto food stored in the fridge below it such as a cake or bowl of salad resulting in the ready-to-eat food becoming completely contaminated.

Thorough cooking of food is very important as the cooking process kills any harmful bacteria in food. Any bacteria which does manage to survive due to inadequate cooking processes can prove harmful to health.

You can be sure that food is cooked correctly by following the cooking instructions carefully and ensuring that food is piping hot *all the way through*. Meat juices should be checked to ensure that they run clear.

Any food which is being prepared in advance or batch cooked should be cooled and chilled quickly and not left to stand on kitchen work surfaces.

Any food which has been frozen should be defrosted thoroughly in a refrigerator, not on a kitchen counter, and cooked food should be reheated thoroughly and only once.

## Effective hand washing

Washing hands is probably one of the single most effective ways of preventing the spread of illness and never has this been more important than when preparing and cooking food.

Hands should be washed after visiting the toilet, before and after dealing with cuts and grazes, after coughing and sneezing, before preparing food, before eating . . . and so on.

It is very important that you discuss with your children when and why they need to wash their hands and that you encourage them to practice hygienic and healthy procedures at all times.

When teaching children how to wash their hands thoroughly, follow these steps:

- Wet hands thoroughly.
- Add soap. Ideally you should use liquid soap as bars of soap can attract bacteria particularly if they are left to sit in water.
- Vigorously massage both hands with the lather. Start by rubbing palm to palm, then rub right palm over back of left hand and vice versa. Interlace

fingers, massage the back of the fingers and between each finger and thumb; pay particular attention if you wear any rings and either remove and wash them separately or wash underneath whilst they remain on your fingers.

- Rinse hands well, removing all soap.
- Dry hands thoroughly, preferably using a paper towel.

# Your child during their first year

## A good start to healthy eating

The first 12 months of your baby's life are crucial. This is the time when you should be starting to build the foundations for their future health and fitness.

### New parents

Many new parents worry about providing for their baby's nutritional needs. They may be concerned that their child is not getting sufficient nutrients or that they are not gaining enough weight. They may be unsure when to start weaning their baby or when to introduce finger foods.

## Vital nutrition for babies

New-born babies change dramatically with regard to their calorie intake in the first year of life. They begin by needing around 300–350 calories and progress to needing more in the region of 1000 calories by the end of their first year as their bodies grow and develop. Parents learn, in time, to spot the signs which tell them that their child is hungry or satisfied and they are able to modify feeding patterns and the amounts of food they offer accordingly.

Babies grow rapidly in their first year of life and may have even doubled in weight by the time they are around five or six months of age. During the first year of a baby's life there is also significant growth in the brain and it is therefore essential that the right balance of nutrition is achieved in order for the child to grow and develop adequately.

During the first few months of its life a baby needs only one food – milk. The new-born baby can suckle and swallow and should be offered either breast milk or formula milk.

## Breast-feeding

Breast milk has exactly the right composition to meet a baby's nutritional needs and it is for this reason that medical experts strongly recommend that mothers breast-feed their offspring.

### Advantages of breast-feeding

- Breast milk contains all the necessary nutrients needed by the baby and these nutrients are correctly balanced.
- Breast-feeding can be an excellent way for mothers to bond with their babies.
- Breast milk contains antibodies produced by the mother. These antibodies protect the baby against infections when breast-fed for the first two or three days after the birth.
- Breast milk is easily digested and absorbed.
- Feeding on demand is easier when breast-feeding.
- The milk does not require any preparation i.e. measuring or warming.
- Breast-fed babies are less likely to develop food allergies.
- There is no need to sterilise or prepare equipment or bottles.
- Breast-feeding is a cheaper option to formula milk.
- Breast-feeding helps a new mother to regain her pre-pregnancy weight sooner than if she doesn't breast-feed.

- Breast-feeding reduces the mother's risk of developing breast cancer in later years.

Although the list of advantages is quite long it is important to remember that breast-feeding is only beneficial if the mother who is breast-feeding her baby eats a healthy, balanced diet. This is because the mother's diet is imperative to the standard of milk she produces.

### Storing breast milk

If breast milk is expressed to be fed to the baby at a later time either by the mother or someone else it is important that the milk is stored corrcctly to avoid contamination. Breast milk can be stored:

- In a refrigerator for between three and five days. It must be stored at a temperature of 4°C or cooler.
- In the freezer compartment of a refrigerator for up to two weeks.
- In a separate freezer for up to three months.

The best way to store breast milk is in the refrigerator as, although still more beneficial than formula milk, freezing breast milk can alter the protection it provides against disease.

It is also important to remember that the milk produced by mothers in the first few weeks of the baby's life should not be stored for long as this milk will not be suitable for the baby when it reaches three or four months of age. Breast milk which is produced by the mother changes to meet her child's nutritional needs as they grow and develop.

## Bottle-feeding

Not all mothers can, or wish to, breast-feed their babies, and in these cases the baby will need formula milk. Formula milk is made from a mixture of ingredients and comes in either powdered form which will need mixing or liquid form which can be used directly. Both types of formula milk should be offered to the baby in a sterilised bottle.

## Ingredients of formula milk

Formula milk has different constituents from breast milk and some of its ingredients include:

- cow's milk
- fish or vegetable oils
- soya
- synthetic chemicals which supply the baby with vitamins and minerals in order for them to gain the necessary nutrients.

## Advantages of bottle-feeding

Some of the advantages of bottle-feeding are:

- It offers more freedom and flexibility for the mother as fathers and other people can take over the feeding.
- It is easier to see how much milk the baby is getting.
- Formula milk is digested more slowly than breast milk which may lead to some babies requiring fewer feeds.
- Feeding in public is much easier.

## Cow's milk

Young babies should not be given cow's milk as an alternative to breast or formula milk. Cow's milk should not be introduced to a baby's diet until they reach 12 months old unless otherwise instructed by a medical expert. Cow's milk is not a suitable food for babies because there is insufficient iron, or Vitamins A and C, too much protein, and too much salt.

## Weaning

As a baby grows there comes a point when breast or formula milk is not satisfying their hunger needs and at this stage you will need to introduce solid food *gradually* to their diet. This process is known as *weaning*. Signs that it is time to start weaning can be if:

- The baby starts to wake in the night for a feed having previously slept through.
- The baby begins to wake early in the morning crying for a bottle.
- The baby appears unsettled after a milk feed.

### Introducing solid food

The most common age to start weaning a baby is at around five to six months although it is important to remember that all babies are individuals and very large babies may need solid food introduced earlier whilst some babies may be content with just milk for seven or eight months.

When weaning a baby it is important to remember that solid food should be offered in *addition* to milk feeds and not take the place of them. Milk should still account for around 40 per cent of a baby's intake even at the age of 12 months.

Between the ages of five and six months babies begin to learn how to chew in addition to sucking and generally they will be receptive to new tastes making it easy for you to introduce different flavours.

## How to wean a baby

Start by offering *very small amounts* of soft pureed food on the tip of a sterilised baby spoon. The initial foods offered may vary from country to country and culture to culture depending on which foods are readily available but as a starting point some ideal weaning foods include:

- baby rice
- banana
- broccoli
- butternut squash
- carrot
- cauliflower
- pear
- potato
- turnip
- yam.

## Increasing food intake

When offering food it is important to introduce water and diluted juice as well. These should be offered in a cup with handles and a lid. Over a number of weeks and months the amount of food offered should be slowly increased so that by the time the child reaches 12 months they are being offered a varied diet of prepared meals during the day which are subsidised with milk feeds at the start and end of each day.

## Introducing new foods

New foods should be offered one at a time with an interval of a few days before offering anything else new so that you can see how your baby copes with the food and whether it has caused any kind of adverse reaction. One of the best ways to do this to avoid confusion is to introduce one new food a week and select a day for doing this. Sometimes a baby may appear to dislike a certain food, however it is important to keep on trying them with it and you should re-introduce the food at subsequent meals.

## Preparing weaning foods

It is important when preparing weaning foods that you do not add any sugar or salt to them nor should these foods include gluten as this can be difficult for young babies to digest.

Although the initial weaning foods will be sloppy and bland you should be continually aiming to introduce a range of textures, tastes and smells so that your child gets used to a varied menu. As the child gets older and teeth begin to show you can introduce more texture to the food, finely chopping rather than pureeing, to the required consistency.

## How much food should you offer a baby?

As a general rule an average 12-month old child should be following these portion guidelines:

- **Fruit** – should be offered in small quantities two to four times a day. A portion may be a plum or half a small apple.
- **Vegetables** – three to five portions, equivalent to a tablespoon each day.
- **Meat, fish** – two to four portions, equivalent to a tablespoon each day.
- **Potato, rice, cereal, bread** – four to six portions, equivalent to one tablespoon or one slice of bread each day.

## Potentially harmful foods for babies

There are some foods which should not be offered to babies as these can be harmful and you should bear the following in mind:

- Never offer shellfish, liver, citrus fruits, raw eggs or soft and unpasteurised cheeses to babies.
- Never give babies or children under the age of three years nuts. In addition to the obvious choking threat there is evidence that they can trigger allergies in some children.
- Never give cow's milk to children under one year old unless it is introduced in the form of rice pudding, custard etc.
- Never add salt or sugar to foods prepared for babies.
- Never give soya-based milks unless advised by a medical expert.
- Avoid giving babies honey as it can carry harmful germs and has a high sugar content.
- Avoid sweets, chocolate, cakes and biscuits when preparing meals for babies.
- Avoid flavoured milk drinks, fizzy drinks and squashes as these reduce appetite and contain high levels of sugar.
- Avoid wheat-based products for babies under six months old.
- Avoid offering too much fibre.

# The overweight baby

Everyone loves a chubby baby. However it is important to keep track of your baby's weight gain and ensure that they are getting sufficient activity. If your doctor or health visitor tells you that your baby is becoming *overweight* it is important that you pay attention and heed this warning. Allowing your child to become overweight early in their development will make them more likely to suffer weight problems in later life and for this reason it is imperative that you think carefully about your baby's diet and exercise.

### Diets for babies

If you fear that your baby may be gaining too much weight talk to your doctor or health visitor and seek their professional advice. It can be very dangerous to put your baby on a diet and you should never be tempted to reduce or restrict their feeds without seeking advice.

An overweight baby may not necessarily be feeding too much. Not being sufficiently active enough is also a major contributor. Many parents will place their child in a playpen, highchair or car seat without considering the length of time they are sat there and this can have a detrimental effect on the amount of exercise the baby is getting. They may not be at the stage where they can run or even walk around but even very young babies need space to explore their surroundings and roll around!

## Finger foods

When you start to wean your baby and begin to introduce solid food it is very important to think carefully about choking hazards. When introducing finger foods a young child will invariably try to cram everything into their mouths as they have not yet learned the importance of biting, chewing and swallowing!

You should always supervise your baby or young child whilst they are eating and choose foods which are *safe*.

### Safe finger foods

Babies around the age of eight or nine months are usually ready to experiment with finger foods. You can make sure that you select the right kinds of food by trying them out yourself. Remember your baby will have few, if any, teeth and therefore the food you offer should dissolve easily or be squashed using the gums. Foods which you may like to try:

- pieces of banana
- well-cooked pasta
- well-cooked vegetables
- fruit which is easy to squash such as a ripe peach or apricot (without the skin). You can use canned fruit but make sure you select varieties which do not have any added sugar.
- shredded cheese
- small pieces of tofu.

## Unsafe finger foods

Avoid introducing the following foods to babies and young children as they pose a choking hazard:

- grapes
- raisins
- cherry tomatoes
- white bread
- hot dog sausages or cocktail sausages
- raw vegetables
- hard fruits
- hard cheese.

# Your child aged one to three years

## Growth rate and calorie intake

The rate of growth for toddlers decreases dramatically in contrast to babies who may grow as much as 8cm in just three months. A toddler, pound for pound, actually requires less calories at 18–24 months than an infant because of this decrease in growth. Many parents are confused about how much food a toddler should eat in order to remain healthy and the table below gives a guide to the size and number of servings needed by an average toddler of 18–36 months in order to remain fit and healthy.

| Food group | Serving per day | Size of serving |
|---|---|---|
| Fruit | Two | 30–60g increase to between 45–85g for toddlers aged 24–36 months |
| Vegetables | Three | 30–60g when cooked increase to 60–115g for toddlers aged 24–36 months |
| Foods containing protein | Two | 15–30g of meat or 1 egg. Increase the amount of meat to 30–55g for toddlers aged 24–36 months; a toddler should be getting approx 1g of protein for each kg of their body weight per day |

| | | |
|---|---|---|
| Dairy products | Two | 240ml of milk or yoghurt and 45g of cheese increase this to 45g of cheese for toddlers aged 24–36 months. |
| Grains | Six | ¼ –½ slice of bread, 30–60g cooked rice or pasta increase this to ½–1 slice of bread and 35–100g of rice or pasta |

### Calorie intake

Generally speaking toddlers need between 1,000 and 1,200 calories per day. These calories should be provided in small meals and snacks. A toddler aged between 12 and 24 months is going through an important transition and is moving from an infant diet which is high in fat to the diet of a toddler which should be giving them only approximately 35 per cent of their daily calories in fat.

## Fussy eaters

Many toddlers between the ages of 1 and 3 years become 'fussy eaters'. This is when they begin to express their independence through what they eat and do not eat and often mealtimes can seem like a battle. Some children of this age group may refuse to try new foods or, if they do agree to taste something different, they will invariably reject it. Toddlers can become 'fixed' on certain foods and demand one particular meal day after day.

## Vital nutrition for toddlers

As a parent it is your job not only to provide your child with adequate food but to ensure that the food you do provide is *nutritious*. By introducing nutritious food early on in a child's diet you will be ensuring that they are less likely to reject these foods in later life. It is essential that you introduce healthy foods from the start rather than at a later date by which time the child may have already developed a taste for sweet or fattening foods and reject those which provide them with the essential nutrients they need to grow up strong and healthy.

## Children's preferences and eating habits

Children's food preferences change regularly and it is always a good idea to reintroduce foods which have earlier been rejected as, quite often, a child will like them second or third time around! Set a good example yourself by eating lots of healthy foods such as fruits and vegetables and minimising your own intake of biscuits and cakes.

## Refusing to eat

Some children worry their parents by refusing to eat certain foods or indeed refusing to eat anything at all. Rest assured that children will not starve themselves if they choose to skip a meal let them – they may simply not be hungry and it is important that you respect this in order for the child to be able to respond to their own hunger cues and not to eat simply because the food is in front of them. Learning to respond to hunger cues is vital if children are to learn the important skill of maintaining a healthy weight.

Having said this, children should be taught to eat at proper mealtimes and with sensible time intervals between meals rather than being allowed to eat on demand throughout the day. Structured meals and snacks are important and these are the times when your child should be allowed to choose whether or not to eat. If they eat breakfast but refuse a snack, let them – however do not allow them to eat anything else until lunch. This will enable them to develop a healthy eating pattern.

## Feeding themselves

Toddlers love to feed themselves and, despite the mess they make, they should be allowed to do this whenever possible. You should always supervise children when they are eating or drinking and be on hand to assist if necessary. Usually a toddler will begin feeding themselves with finger foods which are easy to chew, such as pieces of toast or bread, small pieces of fruit etc., after which they will progress on to using a spoon and fork.

In order to minimise the mess made by toddlers feeding themselves remember to:

- Provide them with child-sized cutlery which they can easily handle.
- Place a plastic mat on the floor underneath where the child is sitting to protect the carpet.
- Use bibs.
- Have a damp cloth handy!

## Keeping your toddler active

Between the ages of one and three most children are very active. They appear to have boundless energy and see no reason not to be on the go all day, every day, often exhausting their parents. By the age of 12 months if your baby isn't already walking they will most certainly be crawling and they will be spending their time indulging their inquisitive nature.

### Restricting toddlers

Although play pens have their uses now is not the age to be restricting your toddler for lengthy periods of time. It may be hard work keeping an eye on them all the time to ensure their safety but restricting them for hours at a time in a play pen is not the answer to this problem. Children need to be active in a safe and secure environment with adequate supervision.

## Finding independence

Between the ages of one and three years children are beginning to leave their baby months behind and are discovering a new-found independence brought about by the ability to walk, run, climb and explore. Parents should allow their children this independence, in reasonable amounts, and nurture their need to discover things for themselves.

## Building on progress

Toddlers will master certain skills at their own rate which is why all children learn to sit, stand, crawl and walk in their own time and each of these milestones may be achieved at a vastly differing rate. What is certain though is that, once one skill has been mastered, the child will progress onto the next – leading to more and more complex physical tasks.

Some children in this age group may become frustrated through the inability to be able to do some of the physical tasks they would like to do. Most toddlers have a powerful motivation and it will not be sufficient for them to be told they can't do something because they are not tall enough, strong enough or old enough. Supporting your child when they are trying to catch or kick a ball and offering them assistance when they are attempting to master these difficult tasks will make all the difference to their progress.

## Making exercise fun

Try not to expect too much from your toddler. Many children aged between one and three years appear clumsy with little muscle control. This is not something to worry about. With practice and regular suitable exercise your child's co-ordination skills, balance and muscle control will improve greatly. Above all else exercise for all children must be fun.

## Toddler skills one to two years

It is important to be aware of the types of skills a child should be able to master at certain ages. Once again these are not set in stone because, as I have already said, all children will develop at their own rate. However most toddlers aged between 12 and 24 months should be able to:

- Walk independently
- Crouch down to pick an object up and get back to a standing position independently
- Carry an object whilst walking without dropping it
- Negotiate steps – though this may well be with both feet together
- Walk backwards
- Run cautiously
- Kick a ball
- Throw a ball underhand.

## Toddler skills two to three years

As your child gets a little older they will have learned new skills and their hand/ eye co-ordination will have greatly improved allowing them to be able to:

- Run confidently
- Walk forwards, backwards and sideways
- Stand on one foot for several seconds
- Climb
- Bend over to pick up an object easily without wobbling or falling over
- Jump
- Negotiate steps with alternate feet

- Kick a ball
- Throw a ball overhand
- Pedal a tricycle.

## Suitable activities for toddlers

It is sensible to expect toddlers to get at least 30 minutes of physical activity a day. This should not be difficult as most toddlers are on the go for much longer than this! Older toddlers between the ages of two and three benefit from physical exercise such as playing in the garden, kicking a ball in the park, going for a walk or riding a tricycle.

## Limiting television viewing

There are lots of television programmes aimed at toddlers, however it is important that parents limit the amount of hours spent in front of the television. There is, of course, nothing wrong with allowing your child to watch *some* television in order to wind down and take time out for a rest but it is a good idea to use television viewing sparingly. Quiet times can be enjoyed reading stories, doing a jigsaw puzzle together or simply sitting and talking.

# 18 Your child aged three to five years

## Vital nutrition for pre-school children

Pre-school children need some important components to ensure that their diet is healthy and balanced. Pre-school children typically eat between 1,200–1,600 calories per day with a steady increase of about 100 calories per year between the ages of two and five years. Their growth at this age is slow and steady rather than fast as in the early years.

## Meal-time battles

The ages of three to five years are typically the times when meals can be a battle with children often refusing to try out new foods. It is important that adults realise how to present food so that it is both attractive and appealing, making the child *want* to taste it. Many recipe books written for children take this into account and you may have seen recipes which encourage making faces from food to make the meals more appealing for young children – everything is worth a try!

### Planning mealtimes

It is essential that adults work on table manners for children between these ages – without making meal times a battle field – encourage children to hold cutlery correctly and explain the importance of table manners.

It is important for children to:

- Be offered a variety of foods – even those which have been rejected in the past.
- Be involved in meal planning and preparation – even young children can be given jobs which they will enjoy when preparing meals for example washing the lettuce or buttering the bread.
- Eat regular meals and snacks.
- Sit at the dining table with the family and eat meals together – this is vital for both healthy eating and for encouraging table manners.

## Adequate diet for a pre-school child

The average pre-school-age child will eat three meals a day with perhaps two or three snacks in between. However, given the chance, they would probably eat all day long, picking at food when they are bored. This is not a good idea as the child who is allowed to feed continuously will never actually feel hungry as they are having their appetite curbed by being allowed to snack all the time. In order to be able to regulate the amount of food we eat it is essential that we know when we are hungry and when we are full.

## Keeping your pre-school child active

Pre-school children should have at least an hour of physical exercise every day. As with toddlers this is not difficult to achieve as most pre-school children will be engaged in play for the majority of the time and much of this free play will be energetic. By adding a little structured play you will easily be able to introduce physical activity to their regime with relative ease.

### Types of physical exercise

You will be able to introduce more complicated physical games to children of this age group as they are likely to be able to understand and follow simple rules.

Most will enjoy playing simple games such as 'tag', 'hide and seek' and 'follow the leader'. Teaching them how to enjoy physically active games such as 'Simon says', or encouraging them to enjoy music and action rhymes, will all add to the variety of physical exercise you can offer.

## Outdoor exercise

Most pre-school children will enjoy being outdoors and, with the correct clothing, there is no reason why a child cannot enjoy the outdoors in all weather. Waiting for a dry, sunny day in this country before participating in outdoor play will result in a lengthy delay!

Pre-school children will enjoy games which need some amount of skill such as kicking a football, throwing and catching a ball, skipping, riding a tricycle or bicycle, doing handstands and somersaults, balancing, playing hopscotch or enjoying climbing apparatus.

Some will be confident enough to participate in team sports and providing they have simple rules which are easy to follow, these are a good way of introducing young children to more active competitive games. It can however be difficult for some pre-school children to understand rules, particularly if these are complicated, and their lack of attention may make team games hard for them to grasp. It is therefore probably better to resist enrolling them in organised classes at this stage and spend time concentrating on building up their basic skills such as balance, concentration and co-ordination.

## Playground safety

It is all well and good ensuring that your own garden is safe and free from hazards in order for your child to play without risk, but what happens when you take a child to the local playground or for a walk in the woods? It is important that you carry out a preliminary check of the areas *before* allowing your child to play to make sure that there are no obvious potential dangers lurking.

Potential dangers to look for in the local playground include:

- broken glass
- discarded cigarette ends
- syringes
- empty cans and other waste debris
- dog faeces
- spilt food
- blood.

Although playgrounds featuring swings, slides and other apparatus can be very appealing to children and they certainly provide them with lots of exercise it is, unfortunately, a sad fact of our society that some individuals seem hell bent on vandalising these areas and using them as places to hang out, drink alcohol and do drugs. It is for this reason that you must check any outdoor play areas that you are intending to allow a child to have access to. Before allowing your child to use any equipment always:

- Make a thorough check of the immediate area, make sure that there is no broken glass, syringes, dog dirt etc. before allowing the children to play.
- Have a good look at the apparatus for signs of vandalism and, if you are in any doubt, do not let the children go on the equipment.
- Always carry a travel first aid kit with you when you are out and about in case of minor injuries.

## Further afield

Deciding to take your child on a country walk or exploring in the woods is an excellent way of introducing physical exercise to their daily routine, however these places pose a slightly different risk. Although there may not be any equipment to check for wear and tear or vandalism there will be other natural risks to watch out for. If possible stick to tried and tested places, where you can be relatively sure that you and the children will be safe.

Before allowing your child the freedom to play and explore, make a thorough check of the surrounding area. This may not be quite as easy as it is to do in a playground as the grass may be long, making it difficult to spot potential dangers. Once again, check for signs of unsavoury characters who may have been looking for a quiet place to drink. Make sure there are no discarded cans, bottles and so on. Other important things to check for when enjoying the countryside are:

- Nettles, thistles and other weeds which may scratch, sting or itch.
- Dog faeces – dog walkers get everywhere!
- Cow dung and sheep droppings – very much a part of the countryside, but not very pleasant if you sit or stand in it!
- Barbed-wire fences – these can be very dangerous as young children often do not realise how sharp the barbs can be.
- Sharp stones hidden in the grass pose a risk if a child should trip and fall.
- Rivers and streams – these can be very dangerous particularly after a heavy rainfall when the flow of the water may be fast and the level deep. Always supervise children near water.
- Animals – remember that animals are very unpredictable and, if frightened or hurt, they can attack. Teach children the importance of treating all animals with respect and never allow children to go near lambs, foals, calves and so on when the females can be very protective and may be more prone to attack.

## Indoor physical exercise

Although most pre-school children enjoy being outdoors and many refuse to come in whatever the weather, there may be times when it simply is not practical to allow them to play outside when it is particularly dreadful. Physical exercise during these times need not be compromised. It is easy to fall into the trap of using the television or computer as entertainment when the weather is wet but there are many other activities which will keep children entertained whilst maintaining a fit and active lifestyle such as:

- music and dance
- action rhymes
- indoor skittles
- indoor obstacle course using foam balls, boxes, chairs and so on for children to practise weaving in and out of.

# 19 Your child aged six to twelve years

## Vital nutrition for school-aged children

Children between the ages of six and 12 years will probably be making many choices themselves about the type and amount of food they eat, however ultimately the control should be left to adults in order for children to be led into a healthy eating lifestyle. Although treats should be available these should be given seldom and never in place of nutritious, healthy meals.

It is perfectly normal for children to be influenced by their friends' food choices and by advertising campaigns, and eating the odd burger or pizza and indulging in cake and ice cream occasionally will not adversely affect children. However it is when these foods are offered regularly and in place of healthy nutritional choices that the problems begin. Eating healthy foods occasionally cannot compensate for a diet that lacks balance and proper nutrition.

### Calorie intake between six and 12 years of age

The daily calorie intake for children aged between six and 12 is:

- 1,600 to 2,000 calories for a child aged between six and eight years
- 2,000 to 2,500 calories for a child aged between nine and 12 years.

The diet for children of these ages should consist of the following:

| Component | Children 6–8 years | Children 9–12 years |
|---|---|---|
| Carbohydrates | 200–250g | 300g |
| Protein | 22–30g | 30–45g |
| Fat | 48–60g | 60–75g |
| Fibre | 10–15g | 14–17g |

## Meal decisions and preparation

One of the easiest ways to teach children about the importance of healthy eating, and why they need to choose healthy food options, is to involve them in meal decisions and preparations. If you explain to them *why* they can't eat fast food all the time they are more likely to accept your explanation than if you simply deny them the foods they ask for without giving a reason. Invite your child to help you choose menus and to assist in the preparation of the meals so that they can become informed about healthy-eating options together with healthy ways to cook food. Offering healthy foods which they like will make it much easier to encourage your child to follow a healthy diet plan.

## Growth spurts

All children go through a 'growth spurt', usually during the time of puberty, and is, on average, likely to be around 10 to 11 years for girls and 12 to 13 years for boys. During this time, when growth increases, the child needs to increase the amount of calories they eat. In general terms children going through puberty need to increase their daily intake of calories by around 200–300; this amount may need to be increased further if the child is particularly active or sporty as they will inevitably burn up more calories with exercise. Athletic children may need in excess of 2,500 calories per day during their growth spurt period.

In addition to an increase in calories children will also need to increase their calcium intake prior to the onset of puberty. From around the age of nine to 10 years the recommended amount of calcium is around 1,300mg in order to ensure the growth of healthy bones.

## Keeping your school-age child active

Often by school age it is possible to determine whether your child is naturally sporty or not. Whilst some children are naturally athletic and take to physical exercise with ease it has to be said that many others simply are not. They may appear awkward and clumsy and dislike participating in any kind of sports.

### Sporty children versus non-sporty children

There are no hard and fast rules when it comes to physical activity and we should not simply view children as being either 'sporty' or 'non-sporty'. Some children may enjoy gymnastics, for example, but hate team games; others may be enthusiastic about sports but simply aren't good enough to play in a team. Whatever the nature and ability of your child it is important to encourage their sporting ability, be this on a serious or casual level.

Children need to feel worthy at this age and if they consider that their skills are not up to scratch or fear being ridiculed for their sporting ability it may put them off physical exercise altogether. This needs to be avoided at all costs if children are to grow up with a healthy attitude towards physical exercise.

### Walking or cycling to school

Walking or cycling to and from school are excellent forms of exercise which most children don't even realise are doing them good! In today's society where many children attend 'out of area' schools, doing the journey on foot appears to be in decline, largely due to the distances involved. However if your child is within walking or cycling distance resist the urge to drive them to school each morning or give them the bus fare so they can catch the bus. Walking and cycling are both excellent forms of exercise and with a little thought they can be healthy, risk free methods of daily exercise. Make sure that:

- Your child is educated sufficiently in road safety practice.
- Your child's bicycle is properly maintained and that they are kitted out with reflective clothing and a suitable helmet.

- They choose a safe route and that they know the importance of sticking to well-lit roads. Make sure that they are never tempted to walk or cycle through quiet lanes, woods or fields, even if these routes are shorter.
- You show children how and where to cross roads safely, and if there are pedestrian crossings en route make sure that your child knows the importance of using them.
- You ask neighbours or friends along the route to watch out for them.
- If your local school organises a 'walking bus' make sure your child uses this.

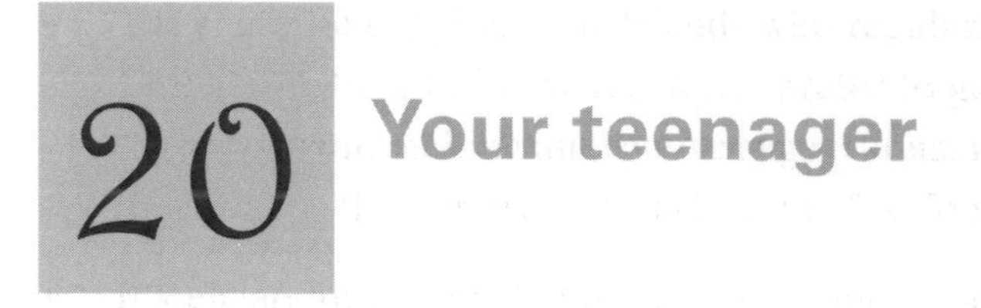

# 20 Your teenager

## Adolescence

Most children will begin to show the first signs of puberty during their early teenage years or just before. As children progress through their teenage years into adulthood it is important that they understand how to take care of themselves in terms of both diet and exercise. Introducing a healthy balanced diet and suitable exercise from an early age should, in theory, encourage your child to choose these options as a matter of routine as they get older and begin to take responsibility for themselves.

Adolescence is a period of rapid growth likened to the rapid growth seen in a child's first year of life. Good nutrition and physical exercise is essential at this time of a child's life. The adults in a child's life will continue to be the most influential role models and it is vital that you are seen to practise healthy eating and take part in adequate exercise if you are to instil the importance of these factors in your child's life.

## Vital nutrition for your teenager

On average teenage girls will require approximately 2,200 calories per day whereas teenage boys will probably need an additional 300–800 calories.

A teenager's diet should consist of the following components:

| Component | Teenage girls | Teenage boys |
| --- | --- | --- |
| Carbohydrates | 300g | 400g |
| Protein | 45–55g | 45–65g |
| Fat | 60–75g | 75–95g |
| Fibre | 18–23g | 18–23g |

Breakfast is vital for children of all ages and particularly for school-age children who need to concentrate. Children who eat a healthy breakfast are:

- more likely to be able to concentrate better in school
- more likely to learn and do better in school
- less likely to consume additional calories throughout the day
- less likely to suffer from iron deficiencies
- less likely to have a higher body mass index (BMI)
- more likely to eat healthily throughout the day
- less likely to rely on snacking
- more likely to be physically active
- less likely to be lethargic.

## Nutritional differences between boys and girls

Although both boys and girls have similar nutritional requirements throughout their younger years this begins to change as they move into later childhood and then more so as they enter adolescence. As their bodies change their intake begins to differ.

**Girls** – When the menstrual cycle begins girls need to increase their iron intake. Girls begin to develop proportionately more fat and less muscle than boys and this in turn gives females a lower metabolic rate than boys.

**Boys** – As boys begin to develop more muscle and their metabolic rate increases they need to increase the amount of calories, protein and calcium they consume.

## Freedom of choice

One of the most important things to remember as a parent of a teenager is that you cannot force things onto them! Teenagers are strong willed and know their own minds – even something as simple as teaching them the importance of healthy eating and leading an active lifestyle may be met with complete apathy. In order to encourage co-operation you will need to continue to set a good example and make sure that your fridge and cupboards are stocked with nutritional, healthy food, thereby reducing the temptation for them to snack on calorie-laden convenience foods which will do them more harm than good.

If your teenager is agreeable it might be a good idea to ask them to go food shopping with you, so that they can have some say in the kinds of foods you buy. If they prefer to leave the supermarket to you then ask for their input before you go shopping.

Allowing them this regular responsibility will help to involve them in the importance of adopting a healthy lifestyle. You may also like to:

- Allow your teenager to cook a meal of their choice on a regular basis, discussing the recipes and ingredients with them before hand.
- Allow them to invite a friend or two over for dinner providing they agree to make the meal themselves and that the menu is a healthy one.

## Keeping teenagers active

In an age of computers and television, encouraging teenagers to become and remain active can be challenging. Many seem to spend their time playing on the play station, the internet or with a mobile telephone leaving little, if any, time for serious physical activity. However physical activity is very important during the teenage years as they are moving from childhood to adulthood and their bodies are changing in response.

Physical activity for the young is easy to incorporate into daily routines as much of it revolves around the need to play. However as your child grows and develops into a teenager it will be necessary to make time and to plan for exercise if it is to be regular and beneficial.

## How much exercise is enough?

In addition to being active – for example walking up and down stairs instead of taking the lift or walking or cycling to and from school instead of opting for a lift in the car or on the bus, teenagers also need to participate in more rigorous exercise at least three times per week. Each of these sessions should last a minimum of 20 minutes and may take the form of:

- swimming
- jogging
- power walking
- gymnastics
- aerobics.

Although many teenagers do not opt to exercise and will often use the excuse of not having enough time to do it regularly, you can help them to stay fit and active by encouraging them to take part in physical exercise which is seen as a recreational pastime rather than a rigid exercise pattern.

## Fun ways of exercising

You could try encouraging your teenager to take up a hobby with a few friends to prevent them from becoming bored with regular exercise. Why not suggest that they spend some time away from traditional sports such as football, and tennis and encourage them to try alternatives which will provide them with just as much physical activity whilst giving them fun and interesting ways to keep fit? They may like to consider:

- horse riding
- ice skating
- skate boarding
- wake boarding
- water skiing
- canoeing
- kickboxing
- karate
- hiking
- mountain biking
- dancing.

The list is endless, and each of these pastimes will provide your teenager with adequate exercise as well as an opportunity to explore new and interesting exercise programmes which can be adapted to suit their own lifestyle and commitments.

## Body image

Many teenagers, and in particular young girls, begin to take a big interest in their looks and their body shape. It is during the teenage years that young people become more self-conscious and they can be easily embarrassed. Although there is nothing wrong with teenagers taking an active interest in their bodies, parents need to make sure that the interest they show is a healthy one and they need to be alert to problems such as excessive dieting, anorexia and bulimia.

## Role models

There is a lot of pressure on teenagers today. Girls' role models are inevitably stick thin; boys are muscular and lean. Many teenagers feel they have to live up to the image of being perfect. Many teenagers are oblivious to the fact that the pictures they see in magazines have often been airbrushed and, even if you explained this to them, they probably wouldn't believe you. Parents would do well to:

- help their teenagers to accept the way they look and appreciate their good points
- encourage their teenagers to talk to them about food and nutrition
- help their teenagers to focus on healthy eating rather than diets
- encourage their teenagers to ignore any advice they hear about fast weight loss and fad diets.

## Anorexia nervosa

Anorexia nervosa is an eating disorder which involves the sufferer starving themselves. Anorexia usually begins in young people around the time of going through puberty. Although anorexia does not just affect teenagers it is true to say that the majority of sufferers are adolescent girls.

Although a person suffering from anorexia will be very thin they convince themselves that they are overweight. Anorexics may use differing techniques in order to lose weight the most common of which are:

- refusing to eat
- resorting to excessive physical exercise
- taking laxatives.

It is thought that anorexia is most common among people who are involved in activities where body weight is considered very important such as dancing, gymnastics and in the theatre.

### *Signs of anorexia*

As a parent of a teenager it is important that you are aware of the symptoms of this disorder which include:

- A body weight which is inconsistent with age, build and height. The body will be very thin and will usually be 15 per cent below the normal weight level.
- Refusing to eat.
- Being obsessive about calorie intake and talking a lot about weight issues.
- The sufferer may be weak and be short of breath.
- Irregular or absent menstrual periods in girls.

Anorexia nervosa is a very serious condition which can result in death if not dealt with quickly and effectively.

## Bulimia nervosa

Bulimia nervosa was diagnosed as an eating disorder in the 1980s. Unlike sufferers of anorexia who will appear very thin and fragile, bulimia sufferers will look perfectly normal. They are usually of an average weight and may even be overweight.

Bulimia is characterised by episodes of binge-eating where sufferers consume unusually large quantities of food, followed by inappropriate methods of weight control known as 'purging'. Purging may include:

- vomiting
- fasting

- excessive use of laxatives
- excessive, compulsive exercising.

Many bulimics suffer from self-loathing however, they are unable to break the cycle of binge-eating and purging which becomes an obsession and which is often repeated. Bulimics are secretive and it can be very difficult to know whether someone is affected by this eating disorder quite simply because binging and purging are done in private. Binge-eating is not carried out in response to excessive hunger, it is usually triggered by depression and stress and sufferers may have very low self-esteem.

### *Signs of bulimia*

Like anorexia, bulimia can affect both males and females. Bulimia is usually associated with professions and hobbies which place a lot of emphasis on body shape, such as dancing and modelling. Bulimia can be difficult to spot as outwardly the sufferer will appear to be of average weight. However some of the symptoms are:

- an uncontrollable urge to eat
- purging (vomiting, fasting and excessive use of laxatives)
- vigorous exercise
- escaping to the bathroom frequently after meals (usually to vomit)
- irregular periods
- constipation
- indigestion
- exhaustion and weakness
- suffering from depression and mood swings.

As with anorexia, bulimia can be treated with the right medical knowledge.

If you suspect that your teenager is suffering from any kind of eating disorder it is imperative that you seek medical advice for them immediately.

## When exercise is at risk of becoming dangerous

We have looked at how some teenagers let physical activity slip due to other commitments or because they simply prefer to watch television or play on their computers. However it is important to look at the other end of the spectrum: at children who go to extremes through their commitment to sport and exercise. These children are often taking risks to improve their performance and endurance which they may not even be aware of such as:

- damaging ligaments, tendons, bones and joints
- risking long-term damage if minor injuries are not given adequate time to heal before exercise takes place again
- exhaustion.

Compulsive exercise is when the participant no longer *chooses* to exercise because their choice has given way to *compulsion*. The person will often feel guilty and anxious if they have not completed their regular exercise regime and they are continuously pushing themselves to improve on their performance.

Compulsive exercise is often linked to those suffering from eating disorders and it is widely believed that people who engage in compulsive exercise do so in order to feel more in control of their own lives, and to deal with emotions such as anger or depression which they do by pushing their body to the limit.

It is important, whilst encouraging your teenager to lead an active lifestyle, to take note of how much exercise they are doing and to look out for the warning signs which may indicate that they are pushing themselves too far in the exercise stakes. Warning signs may include:

- Refusing to skip a workout even if they are tired, injured or ill.

- Losing their sense of enjoyment when exercising because the choice to exercise has made way to a compulsion to exercise.
- Appearing anxious when they have not worked out.
- Working out for lengthy periods of time.
- Working out for twice as long if they have skipped a previous session.
- Appearing pre-occupied with weight loss and exercise programmes.
- Appearing to have lost a lot of weight in a short space of time.
- Allowing exercise to take over at the expense of having a social life or meeting other commitments.
- Never appearing satisfied with their own achievements.

If you recognise any of the warning signs above in your own teenager then you may need to seek professional advice.

As with eating disorders there are no quick fixes to obsessive exercising, however by being aware of when and how your teenager opts to exercise you should be able to keep a track on whether their exercise regime is healthy or bordering on excessive.

# 21 Food allergies and intolerances

Food allergies and intolerances are common in young children although babies who have been breast-fed are less likely to develop these allergies.

In a child with a food allergy the body treats the food in question as a potential 'poison' which triggers certain reactions. These reactions may affect the skin, gastrointestinal tract, the respiratory system or the cardiovascular system and, depending on the severity of the allergy, symptoms may range from a mild rash to a life-threatening reaction known as anaphylactic shock.

In addition to allergies some children may be intolerant to certain foods which, although less severe than allergies, can cause discomfort such as stomach pain or wind.

## Common allergies

Allergies and intolerances are commonly associated with the following food products:

- cow's milk
- peanuts
- eggs
- soya
- kiwi fruit
- sea food.

Children from a family with a history of allergies should be introduced to these foods slowly and with caution. Particular care must be shown to a child who is suffering from any allergy as often traces of food stuffs can be found in pre-packed meals for example, which can cause a severe reaction in a child who is allergic to the food stuff in question.

## Symptoms of allergies

Some of the more common symptoms of an allergic reaction to food include:

- wheezing
- rashes
- swollen lips, tongue, eyes
- puffy face
- anxiety
- fast, weak pulse.

## Anaphylactic shock

Anaphylaxis is a sudden, life-threatening reaction caused by a severe allergic reaction to a particular food or allergen. If not treated immediately a child could lose consciousness. If you suspect your child is suffering from an anaphylactic shock it is vital that you telephone the emergency services immediately. Preventing anaphylaxis is the key for a child who has food allergies. It is paramount that you read all food labels carefully and inform any carers such as teachers, childminders, babysitters, friends or relatives who may be responsible for your child of the allergies your child suffers from in order to prevent this serious form of allergic reaction.

### *Symptoms of anaphylactic shock*

A child suffering from an anaphylactic shock may display one or more of the following symptoms:

- a tightness in the throat making swallowing difficult
- tingling around the mouth
- swollen lips
- wheezing or breathing difficulties
- rapid heartbeat
- low blood pressure
- vomiting
- a rash
- feeling hot and sweaty.

## Preventing allergies

There are many professionals who work with children in order to help them to eat a healthy diet and these professionals include doctors, nurses, dieticians, nutritional therapists, teachers and early years professionals.

We are now increasingly more aware of the need to eat a healthy balanced diet and the importance of providing our children with the same. Schools and early years settings are now very hands on in their approach to providing healthy meals in addition to educating children from a very young age about the importance of eating healthy foods.

## Milk allergies

A child who develops an allergy to milk before the age of three has an 85 per cent chance of growing out of the allergy as they get older. However, children who develop the allergy after the age of three are likely to be prone to the sensitivity for life.

## Common symptoms of milk allergy sufferers

Cow's milk contains over 30 different proteins and it is likely that most children with an allergy to milk will react badly to one or more of these proteins. Many of the proteins are not broken down even when the milk is heated and therefore the child is likely to be allergic to cold milk, heated milk or products containing milk.

Symptoms of cow's milk allergy include:

- rash
- abdominal pain
- bloating
- gas
- diarrhoea
- nausea.

## Foods to avoid with a milk allergy

If you have a child who has been diagnosed as having a milk allergy it is important to avoid feeding them all kinds of milk and foods containing milk or milk products such as:

- liquid milk including evaporated milk
- yoghurt
- cream
- cheese
- ice cream
- chocolate

- butter and margarine
- commercially baked bread, cakes, biscuits etc.

There are many milk alternatives on the market and it is important that children are offered these substitutes, if they suffer from a milk allergy, as they contain an important source of energy, protein, calcium and vitamin D.

## Wheat allergies

Wheat is present in many foods and it is therefore essential that you read the labels carefully to be sure not to accidentally introduce wheat to your child's diet if they are allergic to it. Some of the more common foods to avoid include:

- bread
- crackers
- cereals
- biscuits
- confectionary
- gravy
- sauces
- processed meats such as sausages and burgers.

## Egg allergies

Eggs contain many nutrients including energy, protein, fat and vitamins. However it is usually one of the types of protein which is present in egg white to which some children are allergic.

In some cases the protein which causes the allergic reaction may be broken down when the eggs are cooked and it may be that a child who is allergic to raw eggs can tolerate them in cooked form.

Treating a child who is allergic to raw eggs need not be very difficult providing you prepare foods yourself rather than buy ready-prepared meals which often do not list egg ingredients clearly on labels.

Avoiding eggs on their own should not pose too much of a problem, however it is important to remember that eggs or egg protein are often described differently on prepared foods such as salad dressings and sauces. You need to look out for prepared foods which may list the following words in the ingredients indicating the presence of egg protein in the food:

- albumin
- egg white
- egg yolk
- globulin
- mayonnaise
- egg powder
- egg protein
- frozen egg
- ovalbumin
- ovomucin
- ovovitellin
- livetin
- ovoglobulin
- ovomucoid
- pasteurized egg
- vitellin.

## Caring for a child with an allergy

It is important to keep a record of your child's symptoms both before and after eliminating the food from their diet which you suspect is causing the problem. Record their symptoms and general well-being for a few days beforehand. When you have eliminated the food, continue with the regime for between seven and 21 days and record how your child is responding. Remember that cures are not instant and your child may well feel worse before they begin to improve. It is not uncommon for an allergy sufferer to experience 'withdrawal symptoms' such as headaches and irritability for a couple of days after the food has been removed from their diet but these symptoms should clear up within the first week.

# Nutrition through illness

## The importance of adequate nutrition when ill

Never is good nutrition more important than when a child is ill. Depending on the nature of the illness, one of the most common symptoms is often a lack of appetite. Many parents worry when their child refuses to eat when they are ill and this is understandable as they need to build up their strength to fight the infection and so get better. However it is not the *amount* of food the child eats which is important here it is the *type* of food they eat which will make all the difference.

A child who is ill is under stress. During illness the adrenal glands become deprived of essential nutrients and cannot therefore function properly. The vital vitamins which children require to fight stress and keep them healthy, happy and growing need to be given in abundance when they succumb to illness. These vitamins are:

- vitamin C
- vitamin B6
- folic acid
- pantothenic acid.

# Feeding a child who is ill

## Colds

It is a good idea, when a child is suffering from a cold or fever, to offer a diet which is high in vitamin C and you should offer food 'little but often'. Make small meals so that you don't overwhelm your child as this will help to encourage them to eat. Fluids are absolutely essential to ensure that the child does not become dehydrated so, even if their appetite is low, make sure they are offered drinks regularly.

## Chicken pox

This is a common childhood virus with symptoms such as high temperature and itchy spots. Chicken pox can deplete a child of many essential nutrients and it is therefore important to increase their daily intake of citrus fruits and fruit juices in order to try to counteract this problem.

## Impetigo

This is an infection caused by staphylococcus or streptococcus germs. When a child scratches or picks at a sore such as an insect bite and breaks the skin this allows the germs to enter the body. Children suffering from impetigo may benefit from foods which are rich in vitamins A, C and D. Citrus fruits, milk and fish liver oils are particularly good at fighting this kind of infection.

## Influenza

Every year thousands of children succumb to the flu and, as there are many different strains of the flu virus, it is impossible to build up immunity against them all. Influenza is highly contagious and spreads very quickly in schools, nurseries and so on. Antibiotics are ineffective against the flu virus although if a secondary infection develops an antibiotic may be prescribed. The virus itself, coupled with an antibiotic, will strip the child's system of vital vitamins.

The best protection you can give your child against influenza is a good diet. If your child does succumb to the virus, offer them foods which contain plentiful supplies of vitamins B and C. Foods which are particularly good for children suffering from colds and flu are chicken soup, eggs, yoghurt, ice cream, mashed potatoes and other soft foods which are easy to swallow and digest.

## Measles

Although this virus is now quite rare due to the preventative vaccine which is available, there are some cases where unprotected children succumb to the illness. Measles can affect children differently. Although some children may only experience a mild rash, with little or no fever, others experience more severe symptoms such as a very high temperature and bad cough. A diet consisting of milk, eggs, green vegetables, citrus fruits and juices may be beneficial to help replenish the body's vitamins.

## Tonsillitis

Sore throats and tonsillitis are two of the more common childhood complaints. A child who follows a healthy eating plan with nutritional foods is more likely to resist these illnesses and, if they do suffer from the occasional sore throat, they are usually quick to recover from it. A diet consisting of citrus fruits and juices and plain yoghurt may be beneficial and, because the child may find swallowing painful, you could try offering soups and broths which are high in protein.

## Stomach complaints

It is important to take all complaints of stomach aches seriously as they may indicate the onset of another illness or condition such as appendicitis which will, of course, need urgent medical attention. It is not a good idea to encourage a child to eat if they feel nauseous. A stomach ache usually indicates that the stomach is suffering and it is best not to force food on the child. Allow the stomach to rest whilst continuing to offer liquids.

## Constipation

Many young children suffer from constipation and this is usually because they are not drinking enough fluids to keep their stools regular. Offering foods which are high in fibre will be helpful along with plenty of fresh fruit and vegetables. If you are in any doubt as to how much fibre and fresh produce to feed your child you should consult your doctor, as giving too much may over-stimulate their bowels resulting in stomach cramps. Some good foods to offer children who are suffering from constipation include fresh, unpeeled fruits and vegetables, beans, vegetable soup, bran cereal, shredded wheat and wholewheat bread. You should encourage your child to drink plenty of water and juices such as apple or pear juice.

# Dealing with vomiting and diarrhoea

There are many factors which may cause your child to vomit such as:

- viruses
- bacteria
- difficult to digest foods
- undercooked or badly-prepared foods.

Often vomiting will be accompanied with diarrhoea and children who are suffering from both vomiting and diarrhoea are at risk of becoming dehydrated quickly because of their inability to keep food and fluids in the body.

# Dehydration

Dehydration can occur in a child of any age, however young babies can become dehydrated very quickly and it is therefore important to keep a close eye out for the signs of dehydration if your baby is suffering from vomiting and diarrhoea.

## Common signs of dehydration

The common signs of dehydration include:

- dry mouth and lips
- dry nappies – a sign that the child is not urinating
- dark urine
- irritability
- lack of appetite
- loss of weight
- increased thirst
- eyes which appear sunken
- sunken fontanelle (the soft spot on the skull)
- lack of tears when crying
- skin which does not appear as 'springy' or 'elastic' as usual.

## Preventing dehydration

When a baby or child is suffering from vomiting and diarrhoea they will lose essential fluids from the body and these fluids must be replaced. You will need to encourage your child to drink. Children under the age of two years should be offered water and those older may be able to cope with water, apple juice, tea or sports drinks. You should consult your doctor if the sickness and diarrhoea is particularly bad or very frequent and he may prescribe oral rehydration solutions to replenish the lost body fluids. Oral rehydration solutions contain the right amount of salt, sugar, potassium and other elements which are essential for the body to function properly.

## How much fluid to give

Many parents make the mistake of giving their children too many drinks when they have diarrhoea or are vomiting. If a child is vomiting frequently you need to offer them small but frequent drinks rather than allowing them to drink as much as they like when they like. A good starting point would be to offer a couple of teaspoons or a tablespoon of fluid every five to ten minutes for the first couple of hours increasing this as the vomiting decreases. This will help the child to keep down the fluids. Giving too much fluid all in one serving will result in the child vomiting again once the fluid hits the empty stomach resulting in increased dehydration. It is better to offer little and often to ensure that the body retains the fluid.

## Feeding your child when they have diarrhoea

Although encouraging your child to eat when they are suffering from diarrhoea may initially increase the symptoms it is important to keep offering foods as the body will be able to gain some nutrients from the foods consumed. Encouraging your child to eat through illness will also prevent them from losing too much weight and help them to recover more quickly. However it is important not to offer too much or force a child to eat. Offer small portions of nutritious food which is easy to digest such as chicken broth.

## Feeding your child when they are vomiting

If you suspect your child is vomiting due to a fall or a bang to the head or if their bile has a greenish appearance you should seek medical advice immediately. Do not offer them anything to eat or drink until they have seen a doctor.

If, however, your child is vomiting due to a stomach virus you should offer them something to eat once the symptoms have settled down. You should offer bland foods which are easy to digest. Offer small portions of toast, cereal, fruit or crackers along with sips of water to replace the vital fluids they will have lost through vomiting.

## Medication

Babies and young children should *never* be given medication to stop the vomiting and diarrhoea unless this is prescribed by a doctor. Often the symptoms will only last a day or two and, if they are caused by an infection through food poisoning for example, then vomiting and diarrhoea are the body's way of getting rid of the infection – preventing this may interfere with the body's efforts and prolong the symptoms.

## When to call the doctor

If your baby or child has a very severe case of vomiting and/or diarrhoea, has had a blow to the head, or if they are under the age of two years, then you should consult your doctor for advice. You should also call your doctor if any of the following symptoms are also present:

- a high temperature (higher than 101.4°F/39°C)
- showing signs of dehydration (see signs listed previously)
- vomiting with force
- has been vomiting for more than eight hours
- has blood or slime in the stools
- has blood or slime in the vomit
- is having trouble urinating
- appears to have a stiff neck
- is listless
- is unusually sleepy
- has suffered from stomach pain for more than two hours.

It is essential that you seek medical help immediately if you suspect that your child's vomiting and diarrhoea may be due to them having swallowed something potentially poisonous.

# 23 Unhealthy foods

## Additives

Many years ago when all food was bought fresh and processed in the kitchen additives were unheard of because they were unnecessary. Meals were prepared from scratch each day and eaten the same day therefore the need to preserve food was largely unnecessary. Foods were eaten in season and people did not expect to be able buy fruits and vegetables all year round, as we do today, because this was simply not possible.

However, as our lives have got busier and lifestyles have changed over the years, it has become more and more acceptable to buy ready-made meals and other foods reducing the time needed to prepare and cook on a daily basis.

Although many people still do enjoy baking their own bread, cakes and pies, far more people rely on bakeries and supermarkets to supply these. It has to be understood that these cakes, pies and other foodstuffs are mass produced in factories, perhaps many miles from where they end up, and as such they need to be preserved in order to ensure that they are still fresh several days after they have been made. If you look on the box of a packet of biscuits or a factory produced cake the 'best before' date can be several weeks or even months into the future. The only way it is possible to keep food fresh for this length of time is by using additives.

## What food additives do?

Food additives are needed to help to maintain the taste, appearance and nutritional quality of processed food and to keep it safe – microbiological deterioration can be very high taking into account the length of time it may take for food to be produced, enter the distribution cycle, survive the shelf life, and finally being purchased for consumption. Food additives allow food to be processed in a vast range of brands offering convenience and choice.

## Categories of food additives

The best known additives in food are colours, flavours and preservatives; there are also many other additives each with their own individual purpose. Food additives include:

- **Colours** – Some foods lose their colour during processing. In order to put colour back into the food, colourings are added.
- **Flavours** – Some foods such as soft drinks, ice cream, soups and sauces need many flavours. Flavouring agents are used to impart these flavours into prepared foods.
- **Preservatives** – these are used to protect the food against micro-organisms. Without preservatives food would quickly become spoiled. Some of the preservatives used include calcium propionate in bread and sulphur dioxide in wine and beer.
- **Antioxidants** – these are used to slow down the process of rancidity and the formation of toxic products and loss of nutrition in oils and fats.
- **Gelling, thickening and stabilising agents** – these agents are used to maintain the desired texture and consistency of certain foods such as jam and ice cream. The agents also help to obtain the freeze-thaw stability of frozen foods.
- **Emulsifiers** – these are needed in order to manufacture foods which contain fats, oils and water such as cakes, other bakery products and chocolate.
- **Acids** – are used to add sharpness to flavours, for example phosphoric acid is used in cola drinks.
- **Sweeteners** – Low-calorie foods and drinks have their sugar content replaced with sweeteners which provide the sweetness but without the calories.

## Too much sugar

Sugary foods such as biscuits, cakes, sweets, soft drinks and chocolate are all high in saturated fat and have added sugar. It is advisable to limit these foods to one portion a day. Not only do these foods contribute to tooth decay because of their high sugar content, they are also high in calories. It is important to remember that a high-sugar diet is often associated with obesity.

It is recommended by the World Health Organisation that both adults and children should not get more than 10 per cent of their daily calories from sugar.

### Recommended daily amounts of sugar

Ideally children should not be consuming more than the following amounts of sugar per day:

- Children aged four to six – 40g
- Children aged seven to 15 – 50g.

### Hidden sugar

It is all very well thinking of foods which are high in sugar as also being those associated with a high calorie count such as sweets, cakes, biscuits and chocolate; unfortunately there are many other foods which are high in sugar which are not so obvious.

Foods which we would not usually associate with having a high sugar content, and which are often perceived as being very healthy, are yoghurts, breakfast cereals and baked beans. However if you look closely on the labels of these foods you will see that they contain high levels of added sugar. A bowl of chocolate cereal, for example, may contain as much as three teaspoons of sugar and a small can of baked beans could contain two teaspoons of added sugar. It is therefore important to check labels carefully and, if possible, opt for foods which do not have any added sugar.

## Cutting down on sugar

It has to be said that most children, and for that matter adults, do like sugary foods! By banning sugary foods altogether you risk increasing your child's cravings and bringing on eating problems such as refusing to cooperate at mealtimes or to eat a balanced diet. The important thing to remember here is not to ban sweets, chocolate and cakes but to limit them.

## Tips for helping your child cut down on sugar

In addition to limiting your child's intake of sugary foods and drinks you could try to:

- Read food and drink labels and avoid those which contain 'hidden sugars' such as glucose syrup and dextrose. The basic clues for spotting hidden sugars on labels are to bear in mind that ingredients which end in 'ose' indicate the presence of sugar and that honey, corn syrup, molasses and cane syrup are all types of sugar. Try to choose foods which contain less than 2g of sugar per 100g.
- Resist the temptation to add sugar to foods, for example on breakfast cereals.
- Encourage children to drink plenty of water or fruit juice diluted with water.

# Too much salt

Salt contains sodium and it is sodium which can be detrimental to our health if we consume too much as it can cause raised blood pressure. It is therefore a good idea to avoid eating too much salt whatever our age.

Many processed foods such as breakfast cereals and soups have a high salt content and unfortunately even those which are aimed at children contain unhealthy amounts of salt. It is a good idea to keep a close eye on the amount of salt your child consumes as this will benefit them both now and in the future.

## Recommended daily salt intake

The recommended daily guideline for salt consumption in children is as follows:

- Children under seven – no more than 3g
- Children aged seven to ten – no more than 5g
- Children aged over 11– no more than 6g.

## Cutting down on salt

There are several ways in which you can successfully monitor your child's salt intake and encourage them to eat less salt:

- Check food labels carefully. Opt for foods which contain less than 0.25g of salt per 100g.
- Limit how many tinned foods such as baked beans, spaghetti shapes in tomato sauce and soups you buy as these are often high in both salt and sugar.
- Try making your own soups or removing some of the sauce from baked beans or spaghetti shapes.
- Limit the number of ready-made meals and sauces you buy as, once again, these have a high salt content.
- Limit salty snacks such as crisps and biscuits. Offer healthy alternatives (see Chapter 14 for more information regarding healthy snacking).
- Limit the amount of burgers, sausages and chicken nuggets you serve. These are particular favourites of children, however they are high in salt and one portion may contain as much as half of a child's maximum daily salt intake!

# Fatty foods

Fatty foods are detrimental to children's health. They may provide the body with lots of calories, however they provide very few, if any, nutrients.

Although an adequate fat intake is essential to growth and development – fats fuel the body and enable it to absorb some of the vital vitamins it needs – it is also true that fat has more than twice as many calories as protein or carbohydrates.

## Types of fat

Although we need an adequate amount of fat in our diets in order for the body to function correctly our fat intake needs to be monitored and we should be aware of the different types of fats and what these do. There are three major types of fat: trans fats, saturated fats and unsaturated fats.

### *Trans fats*

These fats are found in commercially-produced snack foods and baked goods. A high intake of trans fats may raise blood cholesterol levels in some people and contribute to heart disease. From 2006 all foods containing trans fats have had it listed on their labels.

### *Saturated fats*

These are found in animal products such as meat, butter, cheese and milk (with the exception of skimmed or non-fat milk). Consuming a high quantity of saturated fats may have the same effect on the body as trans fats, i.e. raise blood cholesterol and increase the risk of heart disease.

### *Unsaturated fats*

These are the fats which are considered beneficial to a healthy heart and are found in plant foods and fish. Three of the healthiest unsaturated fats are:

- **Omega-3 fatty acids** found in oily fish such as salmon and tuna
- **Monounsaturated fats** found in olives, peanuts and avocados
- **Polyunsaturated fats** found in most vegetable oils.

## Fizzy drinks

The best drink for children is water. Unfortunately many children are adverse to drinking water, preferring the much less healthy option of fizzy pop. Fizzy drinks contain many empty calories and often go hand in hand with junk foods which are high in calories and fat. Manufacturers who aim fast food and junk food snacks at children often pair these with fizzy drinks which is why it is natural for children to associate the two together.

### Drink calorie count

If we look at the table below it is easy to see which drinks are high in calories, with a high sugar content, and which are not. However it is important not just to look at the calorie count but to think of the nutritional value of the drinks when comparing them. For example, although milk has the same amount of calories as fizzy pop it is rich in nutrients whereas fizzy pop contains only empty calories.

| Drink type | Quantity | Calorie content | Sugar content |
|---|---|---|---|
| Water | 240 ml | 0 | 0g |
| Low-fat milk | 240 ml | 100 | 11g |
| 100% orange juice | 240 ml | 110 | 22g |
| Fizzy pop | 240 ml | 100 | 27g |

## Takeaways

In a society where many parents work long hours and leisure time is at a premium, more and more households appear to be turning frequently to takeaway meals to ease the pressure on the time needed to shop for, prepare and cook meals. It has to be said that, however convenient takeaway foods may be, they are not a nutritional substitute for freshly-made meals and should not be consumed on a regular basis. Limit your takeaways to special occasions or as the odd treat but refrain from relying on them to regularly put a meal on the table for your family.

Although much will depend on your own eating habits when it comes to feeding your children, if you resist the urge to buy fast food takeaways on a regular basis opting instead to prepare nutritional meals for your children then chances are they will be fine. However the problems arise when your child becomes a teenager and begins to eat more and more often outside the home, becoming vulnerable to temptation. It can be very difficult for teenagers to avoid fast-food restaurants and takeaway shops as these are often situated in the kinds of places where teenagers congregate.

## Reasons why teenagers succumb to the fast-food choice

Eaten occasionally fast food will not have a detrimental effect on your child's health. However, if they replace healthy nutritional meals on a regular basis with hot dogs, burgers and pizzas they are heading for trouble. Some of the main reasons why teenagers opt for fast food include:

- Rushing from school or college to get to work. If they have limited time available they may be tempted to call at the burger bar or fish and chip shop. You can eliminate this temptation by packing them a healthy snack box or suggesting healthier, alternative places to eat.
- If your teenager is at college and staying on campus they may have their food included in the fees they are charged and as such, with unlimited cafeteria food, they risk eating an unhealthy amount of fast food. Although this is difficult to prevent if you are not seeing your child every day, you could try explaining about healthy options and encourage them to make healthy choices when putting together their meals. For example encourage them to opt for a jacket potato and salad some days rather than burgers and chips.

- They may be copying their friends who regularly suggest going for a pizza, Chinese or burger. Many teenagers prefer to go with the majority and will shy away from making alternative suggestions. However it is important that they realise the importance of choosing fast food options *occasionally.*
- It's cheap and tasty! Many teenagers opt for a burger when out shopping with friends or as a quick snack between meals because they are readily available and cheap. However they need to understand that although low in cost these meals are high in calories and fat!

Often a simple lack of parental influence is what puts teenagers at risk when it comes to fast food options. Although it is impossible to prevent your child from ever having a fast food meal you can, whenever possible, keep a check on the amount of fast food they are consuming and be alert to unhealthy changes in their eating habits.

## Tips for fast food orders

If your teenager is eating fast foods you may like to offer them a little of the following advice:

- Make sure your teenager is aware of the 'supersize' portions available and advise them against ordering these.
- Encourage your teenager to opt for healthier drinks than fizzy cola or lemonade which are often served with burgers. Water, diet pop or fresh fruit juices are healthier alternatives.
- Encourage them to consider grilled chicken or vegetarian burgers rather than traditional burgers or other fried sandwiches.
- Encourage them to consider ordering side dishes other than fries. Salad, vegetables or baked beans are a healthier option.
- Encourage them to avoid adding on extras.
- Encourage them to avoid adding lots of mayonnaise, opting instead for low-fat condiments.

# 24 Snacking

## Eating between meals

Snacking itself isn't actually a bad thing *providing* the food we choose to snack on is healthy. Young children in particular are likely to benefit from healthy snacks a couple of times a day in order to prevent them from getting over hungry. Young children's stomachs are small and as such they are often unable to eat large meals and therefore it is not always possible for them to get the energy, calories and nutrients they need through set meals alone.

By avoiding letting children become too hungry, and by providing them with healthy snacks, you can help to keep their blood sugar and energy levels up and improve their concentration span.

What makes snacking dangerous is when children are allowed to snack on foods which are high in calories, sugar, salt and additives such as cakes, sweets, biscuits and crisps.

## Being prepared

The key to healthy snacking for children is to be prepared. If you always have healthy foods in the cupboard or in your handbag when you are out and about, for when they complain that they are hungry, you will be less tempted to give in and buy them a bag of crisps or a packet of sweets.

## Are they really hungry?

The million dollar question! When children say they are hungry do they actually have hunger pangs or is it just something to say? The most important point parents need to establish is whether or not their child is actually hungry just because they say they are.

Children need to be aware of what it actually means to be hungry and this needs to be taken into account when deciding what, if any, snack is offered.

### *Comfort eating*

Many children will complain of feeling hungry when in fact what they are actually experiencing is not hunger pangs at all. Many pre-school children for example will use the word 'hunger' to express feelings of boredom or sadness. Using food as a relief to these symptoms is a very dangerous habit to get into as it can be very hard to undo at a later date. We are all aware of the phrase 'comfort eating' when many people resort to eating food, often sweet and unhealthy, in answer to underlying problems such as depression, sadness or boredom and this should be avoided at all costs.

It is a wise parent therefore who will gently ask her child a question or two before immediately giving a snack to a child who is complaining of being hungry. Taking the commonsense approach in cases such as these is also worthy of consideration. For example a child who is complaining of being hungry twenty minutes after eating a substantial meal is unlikely to really need food and you could try taking their minds off their 'hunger' pangs by getting them involved with an activity or offering to play with them. Snacking for comfort and to alleviate boredom can all too easily spiral out of control and before long you may have a child on your hands who has problems establishing a connection between hunger and emotional feelings.

## Offering snacks

Just as it is important to ascertain whether or not a child is actually hungry before offering them a snack it is also important not to fall into the trap of inadvertently encouraging a child to eat when they are *not* hungry. Ridiculous as this may sound many parents and indeed child care practitioners in nurseries and pre-schools have set times for snacks. It can be difficult for a child to say no to a snack if they are not hungry if it is expected of them to eat and often many children will end up eating for the sake of it rather than because they feel hungry. Although this is not particularly harmful if the snack is a healthy one (in schools and nurseries snacks are likely to be fruit) it does discourage children from learning to say no to food when they are not hungry.

It is a good idea then to offer healthy snacks to a child only when you have ascertained that they are in fact hungry and to help them to understand that it is perfectly all right for them to refuse snacks when they do not feel hungry. By doing this you will encourage your child to have a healthy response to their hunger cues.

## Snacking before meals

Although we have ascertained that it is a better idea to allow children to have snacks throughout the day than become over hungry, particularly if you eat your dinner in the evening and children have to wait several hours after finishing school, it is a good idea to encourage your child to ask before helping themselves to snacks for several reasons:

- You can decide what they eat.
- You can decide how much they eat.
- You can decide whether the evening meal is almost ready – it may be better for your child not to have a snack.
- You can keep track on how many snacks your child eats throughout the day.

### Hungry after school?

If your child regularly appears to be 'starving' when they get home from school and desperate for something to snack on you would be wise to look into what they are eating during the day. If you provide them with a lunch box always check that the contents have been eaten. If your child takes lunch money to school you need to ascertain whether they are actually spending this on lunch or on something else. It may of course just mean that they need more to eat so you could try adding something more substantial to their lunch box or offering them more lunch money.

## Foods to avoid snacking on

If children are encouraged to eat a substantial healthy breakfast they are less likely to resort to snacking at school. The main problem with snacks served at school snack bars and vending machines is that they are often lacking in nutritional value. A high percentage of schools (particularly high schools) have vending machines and these allow children easy access to cheap, convenient foods which are usually high in salt and sugar such as crisps, confectionary and fizzy drinks.

Talk to your child about the kinds of foods you would like them to snack on and explain your reasons behind this. If children are aware of why you prefer them to choose healthy options and why they need to avoid chocolate bars, cakes, sweets and crisps they are more likely to heed your advice.

## Healthy foods for snacks

Think about the types of foods you make available to snack on and ensure that these are healthy and nutritious rather than being full of empty calories which curb the appetite and ultimately make set mealtimes a problem.

## Examples of healthy snacks

Below is a list of healthy foods which you might like to offer your child as snacks:

- raw fresh fruit such as apples, bananas, melon, grapes, pineapple, pears, oranges, nectarines, peaches and berries. You may like to prepare a fruit salad consisting of several of your child's favourite fruits to make the snack more appealing.
- raw fresh vegetables such as carrot sticks, celery sticks and cucumber
- dried fruits such as apricots and raisins
- low-fat fruit yoghurts
- breakfast cereals (check that these are low in salt and sugar)
- smoothies or milkshakes.

# 25 Overweight children

## Body Mass Index

Body Mass Index is a combination of the measurements of a person's height and weight which are used to calculate whether that person is under- or over-weight. It is important to ascertain if a person is a healthy weight for their height.

In order to work out a person's Body Mass Index (BMI) you will need to know:

- Their height in metres
- Their weight in kilograms

You need to divide their weight by their height squared (this means multiplying it by itself).

For example a person weighing 50 kg who is 1.40m tall would have a BMI of:

$$\frac{50}{1.40 \times 1.40} = \frac{50}{1.96} = 25.5 \text{ (BMI)}$$

By using the following chart you can see that this person falls into the overweight category.

| CLASSIFICATION | BODY MASS INDEX |
|---|---|
| Underweight | < 18.5 |
| Normal | 18.5 – 24.9 |
| Overweight | 25 – 29.9 |
| Obese | 30 + |

Children who become overweight suffer several consequences:

- social
- emotional
- medical.

## Social consequences

Many overweight children find that they are bullied or ignored. They are often perceived as being 'different' from their peers and as such others tend to shy away from forging friendships with them.

The fact that an overweight child may be embarrassed or have difficulty keeping up with their peers will often make them reluctant to participate in exercise, adding to their existing problems.

## Emotional consequences

A lack of friends and an inability to feel accepted for who they are will often result in a child having poor self-esteem and a lack of confidence. These feelings of inadequacy may trigger unacceptable attempts at losing weight quickly such as refusing meals or resorting to extreme diets, both of which can be potentially dangerous to the child's health.

As a parent you need to be aware of the emotional significance of food. This is when food is used as a comfort or reward for children and should be avoided at all costs. To avoid allowing food to take on emotional significance ensure that you do *not*:

- Use food as a means of comfort for your child. Instead give them lots of attention and listen to what they have to say. If they are complaining that they are hungry ask yourself whether this is because of other reasons such as because they are bored or sad. Throwing a bag of sweets at them to stop them complaining is not the answer!
- Use food as a reward as this only reinforces the idea of food as a source of comfort. Instead of being tempted to shower your child with sweets or other unhealthy treats such as burgers and pizzas when they have done particularly well at school, for instance, why not suggest taking them to the cinema or buying them a special gift?

## Medical consequences

High blood pressure, type 2 diabetes and high cholesterol are all health-related consequences of being overweight. Although the risk of cardiovascular disease is in adults, the problems of overweight adults usually stem from a poor diet in childhood.

Children who are overweight are more likely to grow into overweight adults, and adults who carry excess weight are more prone to an increased risk in heart attack and stroke.

## Encouraging a change in lifestyle

Sometimes one minute young children appear stick thin and energetic; the next they have developed to spotty, lazy teenagers who appear to be carrying an excess amount of weight! One thing is for sure though that this change does not happen overnight and you need to be vigilant of your child's change in lifestyle and do something about it if you feel they are not getting enough exercise or eating the wrong kind of food. Ignoring the problem will not make it go away, nor will leaving teenagers to their own devices, hoping they will see the error of their ways and rectify things before it gets too late. Chances are they won't see the problem either until they have become overweight and are short of breath!

### Work as a family unit

Try to look at health and nutrition in the family as being everyone's responsibility. Don't lay down rules and expect everyone to conform to your way of doing things; offer suggestions and encouragement.

Make time as a family to sit down regularly together for meals. Ensure the time is relaxed and take the opportunity to catch up with each other's news and share the day's events. Relaxed, sociable mealtimes will be much more enjoyable and children will have a better chance to eat a healthy meal rather than grab something on the move or comfort eat in front of the television.

Encourage regular exercise and take note of any changes in your child's eating habits and body weight, taking particular notice during the adolescent stage where many young people start to pile on the pounds. If not kept in check this is when children can put on weight which they may find difficult to lose.

## What to do if your child is overweight

If you encourage your child to lead an active lifestyle and provide them with balanced, nutritious meals chances are they will remain fit and healthy. If, however, your child has succumbed to poor eating habits and suffers from a lack of exercise they may well become overweight and unfit. If you have a child in the latter category you will need to seek medical advice.

### Medical advice

It is never a good idea to put a child on a diet without seeking medical advice even if it is clear that they need to lose weight. A poor or badly-constructed diet can have serious consequences for a child.

Your doctor will be able to evaluate the severity of any weight problem and he or she will be able to advise you with regard to a suitable course of action. This may involve a carefully-controlled diet plan or recommendations for exercise or a combination of the two. Your doctor may even refer you and your child to a dietician if it is felt that advice on suitable meals is required.

There is nothing to be ashamed of in seeking help. An overweight child is at risk of serious health problems in later life and the sooner the problems are sorted out the better.

## Encouraging exercise

There is no point in pretending that it will be easy for you to persuade your overweight child to take up exercise. If exercise was something they enjoyed to begin with, chances are they wouldn't have become overweight in the first place! However it is important to ensure that they understand the importance of exercise when trying to lose weight. Cutting down on food alone is not enough to lose weight and maintain a healthy lifestyle – it *must* be coupled with an adequate exercise programme.

Physical activity need not be a two-hour workout in the gym four times a week. Many doctors would advise a *gradual* increase in physical activity and some of the changes you might like to discuss with your child are:

- Walking to school rather than taking the bus or getting a lift in the car.
- Learning how to ride a bicycle.
- Exploring the possibility of joining a gym together.
- Starting swimming.
- Organising family exercise such as skating, playing football or other sports, even flying a kite on a windy day!

# 26 Fussy eaters

As a parent it can be very frustrating being faced with a child who refuses to eat properly. All your well-made plans for a healthy balanced diet may feel like a complete waste of time when you serve up a plate of healthy food to be faced by an uncooperative child who refuses to even sample a mouthful. You will understandably worry that your child isn't getting sufficient calories and may even think they will end up malnourished as a result of their refusal to eat.

These kinds of concerns are completely natural and understandable, however they are not sufficient to allow you to give in and feed your child only the kinds of foods they *want* to eat. Children are marvellous at emotional blackmail – if you allow them to be!

One thing for sure is that children do not voluntarily starve themselves! They may refuse to eat the meals offered initially but rest assured, when the hunger sets in they will eat what is on offer. If the food on offer is nutritious and you haven't given into their demands of chips, burgers and pizza at every mealtime then you can be certain they will be eating the right kinds of nutrients they need to fend off hunger, illness and infection. If you do give in to their demands and substitute healthy meals for junk food just to get them to eat, then you will be asking for trouble. Your child will instinctively know that if they hold out long enough they will win you over. Avoid the temptation of giving in from the very beginning and the chances are your children will not become fussy eaters.

## Being a good role model

Children watch and learn from the people around them. It goes without saying therefore that if you are a fussy eater, picking at things on your plate which you are unsure of, or refusing to try something new, the chances are your child will be the same.

To avoid children becoming fussy eaters the trick is to offer a wide variety of foods regularly from a young age so that they will get used to trying out new foods often and not be reluctant to sway from the foods they know.

Your child may well like carrots and peas, however it would be foolish to give only these vegetables and not offer a variety of others. If you introduce broccoli and they don't eat it, don't write it off completely but try offering it again a week or so later; chances are second or third time around they will eat it.

## Personal preferences

Parents often fall into the trap of only cooking what *they* like. Although it is easier to cook food which everyone enjoys it is rather unfair to prevent your child from trying a food which may well become a firm favourite simply because you are cooking and don't like it.

I have been surprised when talking to children of eight, nine and ten years of age who have never tried popular dishes which I have taken for granted that everyone would know about. On further investigation it turns out that the most common reason why children are unaware of certain foods is because their parents do not like them and therefore considering cooking them is not an option.

## Young children

Most toddlers will go through a stage of fussy eating. Although frustrating, it is important to remember that this is perfectly normal in children as young as two and three when they are beginning to have very clear opinions on what they like and don't like. It is, however, important to remember that their likes and dislikes at this age often change and refusing a food one day does not mean they won't eat it a couple of days later. The key here is to offer foods regularly, even if your child doesn't always eat them.

### Older children

Fussy eating habits are not just confined to toddlers. If you allow children to dictate what they will and will not eat at an early age chances are you will be setting yourself up for years of frustration and arguments at mealtimes. Tackle the problems of fussy eating as soon as the issues arise to avoid prolonging them. If you refuse to be drawn in by a fussy eater they should quickly grow out of it and mealtimes will become enjoyable social events again.

## Building up an appetite

This may seem ridiculous but how many parents have been guilty of labelling their child as a fussy eater because they have refused to eat a meal when in fact instead of being fussy they are simply not hungry?

If your child is not hungry, chances are they won't eat food for the sake of it unless it is something they really enjoy – often junk food. If you offer a child a plate of vegetables and they are not hungry they won't eat it, however if you offer them a bowl of ice cream or a piece of chocolate cake the plate will be cleared immediately and this makes some parents think they have a fussy eater on their hands rather than a child who is simple choosing what to eat because they aren't really hungry.

You need to build up your child's appetite if you have any chance of getting them to eat a good meal. To do this you need to think carefully about the time of day you intend to serve the main meal and limit what your child eats an hour or two before the meal is to be served. If your child complains they are hungry a couple of hours before a meal allow them to snack on fruit.

Limit the amount of time your child spends in front of the television and ensure that they get plenty of fresh air and exercise which will do wonders for increasing their appetite. A brisk walk or a runabout in the park or garden half an hour before dinner is served is an excellent way of building up a child's appetite and you will be surprised at how less fussy children are when they are really hungry!

## Strategies for dealing with fussy eaters

It has to be said that fussy eaters can make mealtimes a nightmare and the longer the fussiness continues the more stressful mealtimes become. Parents of fussy eaters often struggle to find a solution to the problem, turning what should be an enjoyable social occasion into battlefield.

You might like to try some of the following tips if you have a fussy eater:

### Exercise

As mentioned previously, encourage your child to become more active in order to build up their appetite.

### Portion sizes

Don't offer your child too much. A large pile of food on a plate can be very off-putting for young children. If you serve manageable portion sizes which your child feels comfortable with they are more likely to attempt to eat, whereas a huge serving may put them off completely. Remember they can always have more if they are still hungry! Cut food up into manageable pieces so that children can feed themselves easily.

### Make food fun

You will be surprised how many children will eat food if it is arranged on the plate imaginatively. Try making faces using cabbage for hair, peas for eyes, carrots for the nose etc. It is possible to get children to eat vegetables and other nutritious food by arranging it in fun ways.

### Keep smiling

Make meal times happy, sociable events. Get the whole family to eat together whenever possible and talk about happy, positive events. Don't get cross with your child if they refuse to eat or appear to be messing about with their food. Patience is very important. Explain to your child that there are no alternatives and, if they don't try the food, they will not get anything else until the next meal time.

## Don't bargain

Although very common practice and something I myself have been guilty of in the past, bargaining using food is not a good idea. By telling your child that they can have a pudding if they eat their dinner you are inadvertently giving them the impression that the food they are being coaxed into eating is indeed awful and the pudding is the prize for eating it! Reinforcing the dislike of the refused food by offering a bargain in this way is not a good idea.

## Encourage but don't force

There is a difference between encouraging your child to try a food and forcing them to eat it. Forcing a child to eat food through spoon feeding or threats is unacceptable. Give your child ample time to change their mind and if after, say, half an hour, they still have not eaten the meal, remove it without a fuss and refuse to give into their demands for food until the next meal is served.

## Offer choices

Compromise is important in most things and mealtimes are no exception. You may be surprised how co-operative a child can be if they have been allowed a choice when it comes to food. Instead of forcing two or three vegetables on them for instance, and watching them refuse all of them, why not offer a choice? If they choose their own vegetables they are more likely to eat what they have selected.

## Limit snacks

It makes sense, but allowing a child who refuses to eat proper meals to fill up on snacks later is asking for trouble. If you do have a lengthy wait between meals and snacking is unavoidable, offer healthy foods such as fruit and yoghurt rather than appetite-curbing cakes and biscuits.

## Involvement

Encourage your children to help you to plan, shop for and prepare meals. Many young children love to cook and by involving them in some of the decision making and cooking you will be encouraging them to eat. By increasing their interest in this way you will be adding to their knowledge of healthy eating and they are much more likely to eat meals which they have had a hand in preparing.

Likewise, if you put food in serving dishes on the table and allow children to help themselves rather than giving them a plate you have filled for them, you will encourage them to judge how much they are likely to eat. They may of course get portion sizes wrong to begin with but they will soon learn to judge how many potatoes they can eat and how much broccoli they like.

# Organic food v conventional food

## What's in the food we eat?

Many of us are completely oblivious to the number of pesticides and chemicals in the foods we eat today. Although much has been made in recent years of the safety of some of these pesticides and chemicals it has become an acceptable method of farming. Modern agricultural practices have allowed farmers to make huge gains in the quantity of food they are able to produce, enabling consumers to purchase food much more cheaply, but what about the quality of the food?

It is impossible, as yet, to determine whether modern agricultural practices are having an effect on our health, and to what degree. What is certain is that many parents across the globe worry about the safety of some pesticides and chemicals for human consumption and as such are increasingly turning to organic foods.

## Organic food

We now know what is used in conventional farming but what exactly is organic food and is it really safer than conventional food?

Organic food is produced without the use of pesticides, antibiotics or growth hormones and has, for safety reasons, become very popular. However it is important to bear in mind that although pesticides and chemicals may not be *deliberately* used in the production of organic food it cannot be completely isolated and often even organic food may still contain traces of pollutants beyond the farmer's control.

## Are organic foods worth the extra cost?

The crux of this question, I believe, is purely down to preference. Many people will argue that taste alone makes organic food worth the extra cost, others would argue that there have been no proven nutritional benefits of organic food over conventional food.

What is clear, however, is that organic food is more expensive to buy than conventional food, and this factor may make organic food a less-appealing option for some parents. Conventional farming techniques certainly make farming more efficient and in some cases conventional farming can make food up to 40 per cent cheaper than organic production.

It is also worth bearing in mind that there are strict regulations on the levels of chemicals and pesticides which are used in conventionally-produced foods and these have been determined to be safe for human consumption. The fact that organic food can not be deemed as completely free of any pollutants is also an argument in favour of cheaper, conventionally produced food.

## Growing your own

There is of course no reason why you can't grow your own organic fruit and vegetables, or at least some. If you have the time and space it is relatively easy to plant up a section of your garden as a vegetable plot and add some fruit trees and bushes. Children in particular will enjoy planting and harvesting their own fruit and vegetables and by indulging their curiosity about where food comes from you can add to their knowledge of healthy eating.

Examples of simple crops to grow are:

- strawberries (can be grown in pots or hanging baskets)
- gooseberries
- rhubarb
- tomatoes (can be grown in pots or grow bags)

- cress (very easy for children to grow and can be kept on a windowsill)
- salad leaves
- carrots
- potatoes
- turnips
- fruit trees such as cherries, apple and pear.

Many fruit trees can now be purchased as dwarf varieties; even the smallest of gardens will often have room for a couple.

## Pick your own

If growing your own produce isn't for you than why not get your children involved in 'picking your own'? Many areas around the UK have pick-your-own farms and, when certain crops are in abundance, you can freeze them for use when they are not in season. Pick-your-own strawberries are particularly popular in the UK.

# 28 School meals or packed lunches?

## Are school meals healthy?

Recent controversy over school lunches has increased parents' awareness of how and what children are fed in the school canteen. Despite the fact that school lunches cost in excess of £1.20 per day it has come to light that, in some schools, as little as 37p per child is actually being spent on food. In order to make these vast savings children have been served cheap, processed, and on the whole very unhealthy, foods.

### What is being done?

TV chef Jamie Oliver recently highlighted a need to improve the quality of the school meals being served to children. In September 2006 the Department for Education introduced new food standards to improve the health, behaviour and concentration of pupils in England and a School Food Trust, which is funded partly by the Department for Education and Skills and partly by the Lottery Fund, has been set up to work with schools and parents to improve school meals through the provision of additional training and to fund extra working hours for the cooks responsible for providing our children with their meals.

With strategies in place the government is aiming to ensure that a minimum of 50p per child is spent on providing food in primary schools increasing this to 60p per head in high schools. Some would argue that this amount is still not enough but it is certainly a step in the right direction.

Ofsted has also announced that school food will become part of the school's inspection process and schools will now have to show how they provide healthy meals for children.

## New nutritional standards

The new standards announced by the government for school food are now complete. These standards cover all food sold and served in schools such as:

- school lunches
- breakfast and after school meals
- tuck shops, vending machines, mid-morning and after-school clubs.

Despite the guidelines it has to be said that schools vary enormously with regard to what is on the menu and, as a parent, it is your duty to check out the meals at your child's school to decide for yourself whether they are balanced and nutritional. Most schools nowadays will send menus home for parents to see what is on offer and they will discuss any concerns you may have, so make an appointment to see the head or your child's teacher if you would like to discuss school lunches.

## School meal guidelines

There are strict rules in place about what schools should be providing pupils with for lunch.

### Primary schools

The majority of primary schools will offer one or two main meal choices daily. You should be able to enquire what is on offer each day and many schools print menus for children to take home with them or have a guide in school outlining the week's main dishes.

## High schools

Often high schools will offer a much wider choice of meals and snacks than those which can be found in primary schools. The key for high school pupils is to ensure that they are aware of the nutritional value of meals and to encourage them to choose wisely.

All school meals, whether they are being offered in primary schools or high schools, must meet key standards for healthy eating as outlined below:

- A minimum of two servings of fruit and vegetables must be offered every day. At least one serving should be vegetables or salad and one serving should be fruit.
- A maximum of two portions of deep-fried foods can be served in a single week. These include chips or batter-coated products.
- Manufactured food products for example, chicken nuggets, are only allowed to be served occasionally and they must meet the minimum standards for meat content.
- Manufactured or home-made meat products from each of the following four groups may be served no more than once every two weeks and only then providing the meat products meet the standards for minimum meat content and do not contain any banned offal.

  Group 1 – burger, hamburger, chopped meat, corned meat

  Group 2 – sausages, sausage meat, link, chipolata, luncheon meat

  Group 3 – individual meat pie, meat pudding, Melton Mowbray pie, game pie, Scottish (or Scotch) pie, pasty or pastie, bridie, sausage roll

  Group 4 – any other shaped or coated meat product
- Oily fish should be on the menu at least once every three weeks.
- Free, fresh drinking water should be made available at all times.
- The only drinks permitted during the school day are plain water (still or sparkling) skimmed or semi-skimmed milk, fruit juice or vegetable juice, plain soya, rice or oat drinks enriched with calcium, plain yoghurt drinks

or a combination of the above. Tea, coffee and low calorie hot chocolate are also permitted.

- Salt should not be made available.
- Ketchup, mayonnaise and other condiments should only be available in sachets or individual portions of not more than 10g or 1 teaspoon.

From September 2006 the government banned the following foods from menus in schools in England:

- burgers and sausages made from 'meat slurry' or 'mechanically recovered meat'
- chocolate and chocolate biscuits
- sweets
- snacks available in bags such as crisps and salted nuts.

## What can parents do to ensure a healthy school lunch?

In addition to talking to your child's teacher or the head of the school if you have any questions or concerns about the food being served in school, there are also several other things you can do to monitor whether your child is eating a healthy balanced meal such as :

- Ask your child what was on offer – Is there more than one choice? If so, encourage your child to tell you *everything* they can remember seeing.
- Ask your child what they *actually* ate! What is being offered and what is being eaten is not always the same. Don't be fooled into thinking that your child has actually eaten everything they tell you they saw.
- Enquire how staff monitor how much or how little a child has eaten. Are there any guidelines in school for ensuring that children choose wisely from the food on offer?

- Talk to other parents and find out their views on the school meals.

## Encouraging children to choose healthier options

As outlined above there are now strict guidelines to how often certain foods can be served in schools and the restriction on fried and processed foods has made parents relax a little with regard to the nutritional value of school meals. However it is important to talk to your child and explain to them the reasons behind choosing the healthier options which schools are making available to them. Although we can't expect our children never to choose chips, burgers or hot dogs even if these are only on offer occasionally, by helping them to understand that these foods can be much less damaging to our health if they are not teamed with stodgy puddings and fizzy drinks they should be able to choose a mixture of healthy options to go with a 'treat' and not feel guilty about their choice.

For example if your child chooses a burger, explain to them that by opting for a jacket potato and salad rather than chips to accompany it they are avoiding over-indulging in unhealthy options. A dessert of fresh fruit and yoghurt rather than chocolate sponge and custard is, of course, also a much healthier option.

Try to relax when encouraging children to choose wisely and understand that they will need to have treats some of the time. Occasionally indulging in fried foods and sweet puddings is not going to make your children unhealthy; it is regular consumption of unhealthy options which you should be trying to avoid. Making your child feel guilty about choosing less healthy options once in a while may lead to eating problems and should be avoided at all costs. If you chastise your child for telling you they chose chocolate cake for pudding when you would have preferred them to choose a yoghurt or rice pudding you risk making them deceitful and chances are next time you ask they will tell you what they think you want to hear and not the truth. This kind of deceitfulness will make any health issues in the future much harder to recognise and deal with and could lead to binge eating and dangerous methods of food control such as bulimia.

## Providing your child with a healthy lunch box

If, after weighing up the pros and cons of school lunches and lunch boxes, you decide to go with the latter you will be faced with the dilemma of thinking how to keep the lunch box from becoming boring whilst providing nutritional food which your child will eat.

The advantage of sending your child to school with food you have selected and prepared is that you know what they are eating – but do you? If you send your child to school with a lunch box containing the same sandwich day after day, chances are they will quickly become bored and think of alternative, often unhealthy, things to eat. They may throw the contents of their lunch box away to fool you into thinking they have eaten it whilst filling up on food purchased from vending machines or, in the case of high school students, the local fish and chip shop or bakery!

The trick to making any packed lunch work, whatever the age of your child, is to keep it interesting. If your child knows what is for lunch before they have even opened the lid of their lunch box you can rest assured they will get bored pretty quickly. Packed lunches do not have to be boring. Don't think along the lines of a ham or cheese sandwich, an apple and a carton of fruit juice day after day. It might appear healthy and nutritious but it won't be appetising on day three, let alone day 23!

It can be a struggle to find inspiration on a daily basis for things to pack into a lunch box and, coupled with the mad rush of getting breakfast ready for the family and the need to set off to school and work on time, it can be tempting to throw anything into your child's lunch box. However it is important to ask yourself why you have chosen packed lunches for your child over school lunches and if, as in many cases, this is because you want to be certain that your child is eating a healthy balanced lunch then it is your responsibility to make sure that you provide one!

### How can I provide a healthy lunchbox with contents my child will enjoy?

The trick here is not to leave everything until the last minute. Often households are in a mad rush in the morning with everyone trying to get ready for school and work add to this mayhem the fact that you may have one or more lunches to make and you will be heading for a nervous breakdown within a week.

You need to plan ahead. A suitable timetable for planning lunches is on a weekly basis. Make a list of five different lunches and shop accordingly so that you can be certain that you have the necessary ingredients. Whenever possible prepare your child's packed lunch the evening before and store in the refrigerator overnight. It may be that leftovers from the main meal that evening can be used as lunch box ingredients. For example a slice of cold pizza or pasta salad can be suitably wrapped, stored in the fridge and transferred to the lunch box the next day. By wrapping everything the night before, ready to put into the lunch box in the morning, you will be saving yourself valuable time and not be tempted to resort to packing bags of crisps and boring sandwiches day after day simply because you lack the time to make anything else.

## Lunchbox contents

A lunch box needs to contain sufficient enjoyable food to sustain your child through several hours. The contents need to be filling and provide the energy needed to keep your child alert to participate in learning and play. The food needs to provide for concentration and the right amount of nutrients and calories – no easy feat!

Ideally your child's lunchbox will contain a healthy drink – no fizzy pop – and a portion of fruit and a portion of salad or vegetables each day. Many parents struggle with this as they tend to think of the traditional packed lunch consisting of sandwiches and fail to see how salad and vegetables can be incorporated. Suggestions for drinks and suitable fruit and vegetable contents are outlined below.

## Suggestions for drinks

Fizzy drinks and squashes should be avoided as they contain high levels of sugar and artificial additives. Stick to the following healthy choices:

- water
- milk
- milkshake
- fruit juice
- yoghurt drink.

Milk and milkshakes can be kept chilled in a thermos flask and if you provide fruit juice dilute this whenever possible to one part juice and one part water.

## Suggestions for fruit

An apple a day keeps the doctor away or so the saying goes. It can also result in a very boring lunch box! Avoid giving your child the same fruit day in day out. They will get bored with it and will probably end up throwing it in the bin. Buy a selection of fruits which you know your child likes and rotate these daily. You might like to try smaller fruits which are quick and easy to eat. If you prepare them and store them in a plastic tub so that your child doesn't have the hassle of peeling and coring then chances are they are more likely to eat them. Suggestions are:

- grapes – opt for seedless
- satsuma
- strawberries
- pineapple chunks
- small boxes of dried fruit such as raisins, apricots and apple.

## Suggestions for vegetables

This is where many parents struggle, but vegetables don't have to be cooked and often the nutritional value of raw vegetables is much higher than when they are cooked. You could try adding the following to your child's lunch box:

- carrot sticks
- celery sticks
- cucumber sticks
- pepper sticks.

Children will enjoy these alone or as an accompaniment to homemade cheese dips or hummus. A small salad prepared and stored in a plastic container will also add a bit of variety to the lunch box.

## Suggestions for sandwiches

Who says sandwiches are boring? Probably the children who open their lunchboxes day after day and are faced with ham or cheese on white bread! Be adventurous with your breads and fillings and give your child a pleasant surprise when they sit down to lunch.

Ideally wholemeal and brown bread should be used most of the time. This is because these types of bread contain three times as much fibre and more iron and vitamins than white bread therefore wholemeal and brown breads are healthier options, and release energy more slowly during the day.

However you could try varying these with seeded bread, cheese bread, herb bread or fruit bread for a tasty alternative. Mini pittas, wraps, bagels, muffins and bread rolls are also alternatives which will add variety to lunch boxes.

## Suggestions for fillings

Cheese and ham are very good simply because they are high in protein. However other protein-rich foods you may like to choose include chicken, turkey, cottage cheese, peanut butter, eggs, banana and tuna. Don't think along the lines of filling sandwiches with just one choice; a cheese sandwich for example can be spiced up by adding a little yeast extract such as Marmite and cottage cheese can be mixed with raisins, apricots or celery to add texture and variety.

## Foods to avoid adding to lunch boxes

It can be very tempting to put off-the-shelf snacks in your child's lunchbox or to purchase ready-made all-in-one lunchboxes which are targeted at young children, but these are exactly the kinds of foods you should be avoiding as most contain high levels of saturated fat and salt and very little, if any, fibre and vitamins.

Other foods to avoid putting in lunch boxes include:

- sandwiches with sweet fillings such as jam or chocolate spread
- processed fruit bars – these are high in concentrated sugar and are not a good substitute for fresh fruit
- bags of crisps
- cake, muffins, biscuits etc.
- sweets or chocolate bars
- fizzy drinks.

## Healthy foods suitable for lunchboxes

For variety, and to make your child's lunchbox appetising, try adding some of the following:

- breadsticks
- dried fruit
- nuts such as cashews, almonds, brazils and peanuts (check the school's policy on nuts)
- plain popcorn
- yoghurt.

## The perfect lunchbox

Trying to make the perfect lunchbox is a challenge and not something that every parent can get right every day. However by sticking to the following rules you can be sure that your child's lunchbox will be filled with a healthy balanced meal consisting of the necessary protein, vitamins and nutrients to sustain them throughout the day. Each lunch box should contain:

- a drink
- a portion of fruit, either fresh or dried
- a portion of vegetables or salad
- one protein-rich food such as meat, fish or egg
- one carbohydrate such as bread or pasta
- one dairy food such as cheese or yoghurt.

# Five a day

## Why is it important that children get their 'five a day'?

The World Health Organisation and the UK's Food Standards Agency recommend that we all eat a minimum of five portions of fruit and vegetables every day. However getting children to eat this amount can be struggle. It is estimated that children in the UK only get an average of two portions of fruit and vegetables each day which is, of course, way below the recommended amount.

Fruit and vegetables are a great source of fibre, nutrients and vitamins and are an excellent way of boosting our immune systems and keeping us healthy. It is for these reasons that it is essential that we try to encourage our children to meet the five-a-day guidelines.

## How much is a portion?

Below are some examples of a portion of fruit and vegetables for a child:

### Fruit

- one small apple or orange
- one satsuma, plum or kiwi fruit
- one small peach or nectarine
- approximately ten to 15 grapes

- approximately five to eight strawberries
- two to three tablespoons of tinned fruit in natural juices
- one tablespoon of raisins, sultanas or dried apricots and mangoes
- one slice of melon or fresh pineapple (approximately two inches thick)
- one banana
- one glass of fruit juice
- three to five cherry tomatoes.

### Vegetables

- two tablespoons of peas, sweetcorn or cabbage
- two spears of broccoli
- two florets of cauliflower
- one cooked carrot
- two tablespoons of tinned or frozen vegetables
- two tablespoons of baked beans, butter beans, kidney beans or haricot beans.

It is important to remember that beans can only be counted once towards the five-a-day guidelines no matter how many portions are eaten.

## Achieving five a day

On average a child eating a healthy balanced diet will probably be eating three meals per day along with a couple of snacks to keep them going between meals. The five a day target is easily achieved if one portion of fruit or vegetables is offered at each meal or snack time.

For example five a day can be achieved in the following ways:

**Day One**

| | |
|---|---|
| Breakfast | one tablespoon of raisins added to cereal |
| Snack | ten grapes |
| Lunch | banana and honey sandwich |
| Snack | one apple |
| Dinner | fruit crumble for pudding |

**Day Two**

| | |
|---|---|
| Breakfast | sliced banana added to cereal |
| Snack | glass of fruit juice |
| Lunch | vegetable soup |
| Snack | slice of melon |
| Dinner | portion of carrots |

If you look at the suggestions it is easy to see how you can achieve more than the recommended five-a-day fruit and vegetable portions; offering a glass of fruit juice in addition to fruit with cereal at breakfast time and dinner of two vegetables and a pudding incorporating fruit will provide a minimum of two portions for these meals alone.

Achieving the five-a-day target will not necessarily mean a huge change in the way you cook and prepare food unless of course you and your family are leading a very unhealthy lifestyle at present. Often fruit and vegetables can easily be added to favourite recipes which you may already prepare regularly. For example try adding chopped carrots, courgettes, mushrooms and peppers in addition to the tomatoes you use when preparing sauce for bolognese or other pasta dishes. Stews, casseroles and soups are an excellent way of adding a variety of vegetables and pulses to your child's diet.

## Encouraging your child to eat more fruit and vegetables

We looked at ways of getting children interested in fruit and vegetables in Chapter 27 when it was recommended that children should be involved in growing and harvesting fruit and vegetables and this is an excellent way of encouraging them to eat more healthy produce. Being involved nurtures a child's curiosity and they are more likely to be interested in eating something which they have themselves contributed to growing. Get your children involved in growing vegetables such as runner beans, tomatoes and courgettes which are relatively easy to grow in pots, grow bags or small vegetable plots.

## Variety

Try to provide a variety of fruit and vegetables and keep offering them even if they are not eaten first or second time around. Often young children's tastes and preferences will vary tremendously and you may find that what won't be touched one week will be eagerly devoured the next.

Offer raw vegetables and cooked fruits instead of the traditionally-cooked vegetables and raw fruit. A child who doesn't like the texture of a cooked carrot may well enjoy a crunchy carrot stick and a child who isn't keen on apples might enjoy a spoonful of stewed apple on a rice pudding dessert. The portion, however served, counts towards their five-a-day guideline.

It is sometimes necessary to hide or disguise vegetables in order for children to eat them and this can be done in a number of ways such as:

- Mixing vegetables such as swede, turnip or parsnip into mashed potatoes.
- Adding vegetables other than traditional tomatoes to sauces for pasta dishes, for example mushrooms and broccoli.
- Making faces or patterns from vegetables to make them look more appealing.
- Adding grated cheese to vegetables or a cheese sauce to cauliflower, broccoli or sprouts.

## Setting a good example

It is necessary, as with most things, to set a good example for your children to follow. If they see you reaching for the fruit bowl instead of the biscuit tin when you need a snack they are much more likely to follow suit.

You need to be careful what you say, reiterating at every opportunity that you like salad, fruit and vegetables and never moan about having to eat them just because they are good for you.

## Give your child choices

Try to let your children make their own decisions whenever possible. They are more likely to eat something they have selected rather than something which has been forced on them. This isn't as difficult or as wasteful as it might first appear. If you cook two or three vegetables ask your child which they prefer and use any leftovers to make soups or stews. If you prefer not to cook more vegetables than you may need then ask your child at the preparation stage which vegetables they would like with their dinner. Often, empowering a child in this way to take responsibility for their meals will encourage them to eat. They can hardly moan at not liking something they have chosen themselves!

## Involve children

As mentioned earlier it is a good idea to involve children in the preparation and cooking of meals. Source simple recipes which even the youngest of children can try out, and get them involved in the shopping stage allowing them to make some of the decisions as to what meals to make.

## Add to traditional recipes

It can be easy to encourage children to eat vegetables by adding them to your usual traditional meals. For example, pizza can have a handful of mushrooms or peppers added as an extra topping, prepared soups will benefit from added vegetables, and fresh fruit can be added to milkshakes. The possibilities are endless and with a little imagination you will be able to come up with some effortless ways of introducing more fruit and vegetables into your child's diet.

## Make it colourful

It is important to remember to offer a *variety* of fruit and vegetables in your child's diet. Each fruit and vegetable will provide different health benefits and it is for this reason that you need to ensure that your child isn't eating the same foods every day.

An easy way to ensure a varied diet is to mix the colours of fruits and vegetables. Try to encourage your child to see how many different colours of fruit and vegetables they can eat in a day, as each different coloured food will provide them with different vitamins and nutrients needed for a healthy balanced diet.

### *Red*

Red fruits, including blood oranges, cherries, cranberries, red grapes, red apples, raspberries, strawberries etc., and red vegetables, such as beetroot, radishes and red peppers provide us with nutrients and vitamins which promote a healthy heart.

### *Orange/yellow*

Orange/yellow fruits such as apricots, lemons, mangoes, peaches, papayas, pineapples, yellow pears, cantaloupe melon, grapefruits etc and orange/yellow vegetables including butternut squash, carrots, pumpkin, sweetcorn and yellow peppers may help to reduce the risk of certain cancers if they are included in our diet.

### *Green*

Green fruits, including green apples, grapes, pears, limes and kiwi fruit, and vegetables such as broccoli, cabbage, green beans, spinach, watercress, peas, asparagus and Brussels sprouts provide us with nutrients and vitamins to promote, among other things, good vision.

### *Blue/purple*

Blue/purple fruits such as blackberries, blueberries, bilberries, plums and blackcurrants and vegetables such as purple cabbage and peppers are required to help maintain memory.

### *White*

White fruits such as bananas, white pears and white nectarines along with white vegetables such as cauliflower, parsnips, onion, turnips and mushrooms are needed to promote healthy cholesterol levels.

## Chemicals in fruit and vegetables

Scientists have discovered over 10,000 phytochemicals which are present in fruits and vegetables. It is these phytochemicals, found in plant pigments, which produce the colouring in fruit and vegetables. Each phytochemical plays a unique and specific role in promoting health and it is believed that the overall effect of a low-fat diet rich in fruit and vegetables reduces risk of heart disease, certain types of cancer and other chronic diseases.

# 30 Vegetarian diets

## The vegetarian diet

Generally, people who eat a vegetarian diet are defined as those who refuse to eat meat, preferring instead to consume mainly plant foods such as fruits and vegetables along with grains, seeds and nuts. There are, however, many different types of vegetarians and their diets may differ enormously.

## Types of vegetarians

The most common types of vegetarian are:

- semi- or partial vegetarians
- pesco-vegetarians
- lacto-ovo vegetarians
- vegans.

### Semi- or partial vegetarians

These types of vegetarians vary from those who follow a full vegetarian diet in that although they will generally avoid red meat they may still consume poultry and fish. They do, however, primarily eat vegetarian foods and their diet will largely consist of fruits, vegetables, grains, seeds and nuts.

### Pesco-vegetarians

Pesco-vegetarians avoid all red meat and poultry but still consume fish and/or seafood.

### Lacto-ovo vegetarians

These types of vegetarians refuse to eat all foods derived from animal flesh including meat, poultry and fish. 'Lacto' means that they still consume dairy products and 'ovo' that they will include eggs and egg products in their diet.

### Vegans

The vegan diet is very strict. Vegans avoid all foods of animal origin including meat, poultry, fish, eggs, dairy, gelatine and honey.

## How does a vegetarian diet affect health?

A vegetarian diet may not be to everyone's taste and some people wonder how a diet devoid of meat products can be enjoyed, however research does suggest that there are a number of potential health benefits for sticking to a mainly vegetarian diet. For example those who stick to eating a primarily vegetarian diet are less likely to have high blood pressure or to die from coronary artery disease as their diet is typically lower in saturated fat. Research also suggests that people who follow a vegetarian diet have lower rates of certain types of cancer. Vegetarians are also less likely to suffer from obesity.

## Should children be given a vegetarian diet?

Although the information above would suggest that a vegetarian diet is of benefit to everyone, and as such makes sense for us all to adopt it, it has to be said that vegetarianism is not suitable for everyone; the health benefits of such a diet are only apparent if it is carefully planned so that the right number and amount of nutrients are consumed on a daily basis. Let us not forget that a *varied* balanced diet consisting of meat, fruit, vegetables, diary foods etc. provides us with the essential nutrients and vitamins needed for a healthy life. Take away some of these foods and the potential to deplete important sources of nutrients and vitamins is high.

A carefully-planned vegetarian diet is therefore essential to ensure that it provides all the necessary nutrients and this is particularly so in the case of children who need to be well nourished in order to grow and develop at a normal pace.

## What the body needs

There are certain nutrients which the body requires in order to develop and grow and all of these can be found in a balanced diet. These include:

- protein
- fibre
- iron
- vitamins
- calcium
- zinc.

By taking away meat and, in the case of those following a vegan diet, fish, dairy and egg products, you seriously reduce the sources which provide these essential nutrients. It is therefore necessary to think about how these nutrients can be replenished.

### Energy

Vegetarians who eat mainly plant foods may find that they lack energy. This is because many plant foods are not concentrated sources of calories and as such are usually quite low in energy. Energy levels can be boosted by eating certain plant foods which are high in calories such as avocado and nuts.

## Protein

The body needs nine essential amino acids which our body cannot make itself and which we therefore need to get from the food we eat. Meat contains all nine of these amino acids and so eating meat on a regular basis ensures that the body gets the amino acids it needs from this form of *complete protein*. Vegetarians on the other hand need to find other ways of achieving this as plant proteins are known as *incomplete proteins* because they are missing at least one of the essential amino acids. In order to ensure that adequate sources of protein are consumed, vegetarians need to make sure that they eat plant proteins in combinations which make them complete.

Although this sounds complicated most of us will be consuming a variety of foods, unintentionally, which when eaten separately will be lacking one or more essential amino acids but when eaten together become complete. Examples of this are:

- lentil soup eaten with a bread roll
- baked beans on toast
- milk with breakfast cereal
- bread with cheese
- hummus with pitta bread.

## Fibre

Fibre is not found in meat, only in plant foods. You would think therefore that this would not be a problem for those sticking to a vegetarian diet. However this is not actually the case. Children who are fed on a vegetarian diet have the potential to be deficient in calories which are needed to ensure adequate growth and it is therefore essential that a child on a vegetarian diet has additional concentrated sources of fat added to their diet such as cheese, eggs and nuts.

## Iron

Some of the iron we need, which is easily absorbed by the body, is found in meat. Other types of iron which is found in plant foods is less easy for the body to absorb and therefore children who are fed a vegetarian diet may have difficulty obtaining sufficient iron for the blood cells to function properly. It is important to add plant sources, which are high in iron, to a child's diet and these foods include tofu, leafy green vegetables and prunes. Vitamin C, found in oranges, can aid the absorption of iron in the body.

## Vitamins

Certain vitamins such as vitamin B12 and vitamin D can only be derived from either meat or animal products. A deficiency in these vitamins is of particular concern for those children who consume a vegan diet as both of these vitamins can be derived from milk and/or eggs but a vegan diet avoids both these products and is likely to need boosting with supplements to avoid vitamin deficiency.

## Calcium

Calcium which is derived from milk is generally not a concern for children following a lacto-vegetarian diet as it is likely that they will consume adequate amounts of dairy products to gain the necessary calcium intake required for boosting bone mass during growth. However a child who consumes a vegan diet may well not get enough as the many plants which do contain calcium do so in such small quantities that the foods would have to be consumed in ridiculously large portions to make them effective. As such calcium fortified foods or calcium supplements will probably need to be added to the diet to prevent calcium deficiency.

## Zinc

Unlike many of the other nutrients, children following a vegetarian or vegan diet rarely lack this essential nutrient as zinc is easily obtained from grains and nuts.

## What is tofu?

Tofu is manufactured from soybeans and it is an exceptionally versatile plant-based source of protein. Although rather bland and tasteless if eaten on its own it absorbs the flavour of the food it is cooked with and can be used in a variety of recipes.

### *Types of tofu*

Tofu comes in three main types:

- silken
- soft
- firm.

**Silken tofu** is often used in desserts and soups as it has a cream-like consistency and blends well.

**Soft tofu** is often used in soups. It is less creamy than silken tofu but not as solid and dense as firm tofu.

**Firm tofu** contains the most protein and fat of all three types of tofu and can be grilled or used in stir fries amongst other things.

# Ensuring your vegetarian child eats healthily

Although the best diet for children is one which is balanced and healthy and contains a variety of foods, that is not to say that children who are brought up on a vegetarian diet are unhealthy. It is, however, vital, that plenty of thought is put into a vegetarian diet for children if it is to provide an adequate amount of essential nutrients and vitamins in order to avoid deficiency in any areas.

It should be remembered that the less restrictive the vegetarian diet the easier it will be for your child to get sufficient protein and important nutrients. As such the best type of vegetarian diet for children and teenagers to follow would be the lacto-ovo diet which allows the consumption of dairy products and eggs.

## Tips for eating a healthy vegetarian diet

- Make sure that you provide at least five servings of fruit and vegetables every day in order to provide the essential vitamins and minerals the body requires.
- Always provide foods from all four food groups for vegetarians:
  fruits
  vegetables
  grains
  beans.
- Include protein-rich foods with every meal such as eggs and milk.
- Be careful not to provide too many high fibre foods, and if possible balance these with sources of energy and fat such as dairy products including cheese and yoghurt.
- Make sure that plant foods which are high in iron and zinc are provided on a daily basis.
- Ensure that you include a reliable source of vitamin B12 in the diet which can be gained from milk and eggs.

# 31 Recipes for children

## Babies up to 12 months

Most babies are weaned before the age of twelve months. Ideal weaning foods for babics are purees which can easily be made at home in batches, frozen and stored until required.

If you store pureed baby food in ice cube trays you can choose portion sizes depending on the appetite of your child. For example a child who eats only small amounts of food in addition to their regular milk feeds may only need one ice cube quantity whereas an older baby may require four or five portions.

It is a good idea when freezing purees to label them with their content and expiry date. The guide below will help you to do this.

| Food | Approximate freezer storage times |
| --- | --- |
| Vegetables | Up to six months |
| Fruit | Up to six months |
| Meat and chicken | Up to ten weeks |
| Fish | Up to ten weeks |
| Purees which have been made using milk | Between four to six weeks |

If you look at the chart above you can see that it is possible to prepare several months supply of nutritious baby purees in one session making it much less time consuming.

## Popular recipes for baby purees

The recipes below give suitable variations on purees using foods which are easy for the baby to digest and offer plenty of vitamins and nutrients. If possible try to steam food rather than boil it as boiling tends to destroy many of the important nutrients.

## Broccoli and cauliflower puree

**Ingredients**: 4 large broccoli florets
4 large cauliflower florets

**Method**: Steam the vegetables until they are tender. Puree both vegetables together in a blender using a small amount of cooled boiled water or your baby's usual milk to adjust the texture of the mixture. Allow to cool and transfer to an ice cube tray. Freeze for up to six months if water is used to blend and four to six weeks if you use milk. The above quantities will make approximately four to five servings depending on your child's appetite.

## Potato and spinach puree

**Ingredients**: 4 medium-sized potatoes
100g of spinach

**Method**: Peel, chop and steam the potatoes. If you do boil vegetables then do not add any salt. Steam the spinach. Puree both the potato and the spinach together in a blender adding a little cooled boiled water or your baby's usual milk to adjust the texture. Freeze as detailed earlier. The above quantities will make approximately four to five servings.

## Vegetable medley

**Ingredients**: 4 carrots
2 parsnips
4 Brussels sprouts
3 potatoes

**Method**: Peel, chop and steam all the vegetables. If you prefer to boil them do so over a gentle heat and do not add any salt to the water. Puree all the vegetables together in a blender adding cooled boiled water or a little of your baby's usual milk until you have the desired consistency. Allow to cool and transfer to the ice cube tray. Freeze as outlined above. The quantities used in this recipe will make approximately four to five servings.

## Cod and vegetables

**Ingredients**: 200g of cod fillet, skinned and de-boned
2 medium potatoes
2 carrots
2 large cauliflower florets

**Method**: Peel, chop and steam the vegetables. Steam or grill the cod fillet. Puree the vegetables and the cod fillet together in a blender adding a little cooled boiled water or your baby's usual milk to reach the desired consistency. Allow to cool and transfer to ice cube trays to freeze.

## Pear and apple puree

**Ingredients**: 2 pears
2 apples

**Method**: Peel and slice the fruits and steam or boil gently until the fruit is tender. Puree together in a blender and transfer, when cool, to an ice cube tray. Sufficient for two to three servings.

### Banana puree

**Ingredients**: 1 small banana

**Method**: Puree the banana in a blender and add a little of your baby's usual milk. Serve immediately – banana is not suitable for freezing.

## Toddlers one to three years

### Shepherd's pie

**Ingredients**:

450g of lean minced beef
1 onion peeled and chopped
1 red pepper, cored and diced
1 tablespoon of olive oil
2 carrots, peeled and chopped
1 stick of celery, chopped
6 mushrooms, chopped
1 kg potatoes, peeled and chopped
Splash of milk
Herbs such as parsley, or mixed herbs

**Method**: Steam or boil the potatoes until tender then mash adding the milk to get the required consistency. Heat the oil in a pan and add the onions, cook until tender and add the mince beef. Cook until the meat is brown and add the remaining vegetables and herbs. Cook for a further 15 minutes until all the vegetables are tender. Place the meat mixture into a suitable dish or dishes if you are making individual pies, and add the mashed potatoes on top smoothing over with a fork. Bake in the oven for approximately 20–30 minutes at 180°C/350°F/Gas mark 4 until the potato topping has browned.

### Baked fruit

**Ingredients**: 1 eating apple, cored and chopped
1 pear, cored and chopped
1 orange, peeled, segmented and chopped
1 peach, stoned and chopped
1 banana, peeled and sliced
2 tablespoons of orange juice
Half a teaspoon of cinnamon
3 tablespoons of raisins

**Method**: Place all the fruit in a shallow ovenproof dish. Add the orange juice, pouring all over the fruit to coat it. Sprinkle the raisins and cinnamon over the top, cover with foil and bake in the oven for about 20 minutes or until the fruit is tender. Remove the foil and bake for a further 10-15 minutes to crisp the fruit. This recipe is ideal served with ice-cream as a treat or natural yoghurt as a healthy dessert.

## Pre-school children three to five years

### Beef stew

Beef stew is a simple but healthy dish for active pre-school children which is easy to make and can be served with potatoes, bread or dumplings.

**Ingredients**: 500g of stewing or braising steak, diced
1 tablespoon of olive oil
1 large onion, peeled and chopped
500 ml of beef stock
4 carrots, peeled and chopped
1 small turnip, peeled and chopped
3 sticks of celery, chopped
Herbs

**Method**: Cook the meat in the olive oil until brown. Transfer the meat to an ovenproof, lidded casserole dish and add the vegetables and herbs. Pour over the stock and cover. Cook in the oven for approximately 2 hours at 170°C/325°F/Gas mark 3.

### Fruit crumble

**Ingredients**:
125g plain flour
50g sugar
75g butter, cut into small pieces
Fruit of your choice (for example cooking apples, 3 sticks of rhubarb, 5 pears)

**Method**: Peel, core and slice the fruit and lay in the bottom of an ovenproof dish, sprinkle with 25g of sugar. In a large mixing bowl add the flour and 25g of sugar and mix thoroughly, Add the butter, then, using fingers, rub it into the flour and sugar until it resembles fine breadcrumbs.

Spread the crumble mixture over the fruit making sure that all the fruit is covered and bake in the oven at 180°C/350°F/Gas mark 4 for approximately 30 minutes or until the top of the crumble is golden brown. Fruit crumble is delicious served with ice cream, custard or crème fraiche.

## School-age children five to twelve years

Children of these ages usually love pizzas and, if these are homemade, you will be able to indulge their tastes whilst ensuring that your children are getting fresh ingredients which are both tasty and nutritious.

### Pizza

**Ingredients**: 1 pizza base – these can be purchased ready made or as a dough mix

2 tablespoons of tomato puree
Your child's choice of toppings: this could include chicken, sweetcorn, tuna, ham, cheese, mushrooms, tomatoes etc.

**Method**: Make up the pizza base according to the packet and spread the tomato puree on the base. Add toppings of your choice. Cook in the oven for approximately 20 minutes at 220°C/425°F/Gas mark 7.

### Sweet pancakes

**Ingredients**: 100g plain flour
1 medium egg, beaten
270ml semi-skimmed milk
A little oil to fry with
Fruit of your choice such as sliced banana, cherries, apples etc.

**Method**: Sieve the flour into a mixing bowl and slowly add the egg, beating with a fork or whisk. Gradually add the milk, continuing to mix well before adding more. Add a little oil to a medium frying pan and pour in enough batter mixture to just coat the bottom of the pan. Allow the pancake to cook for a couple of minutes before tossing over to brown the other side. Transfer the pancake to a plate and add sliced banana, grated apple and sultanas or de-stoned cherries. Fold the pancake in half, sprinkle with a little sugar and serve.

## Teenagers

### Chicken and vegetable stir fry

**Ingredients**: 3 chicken breast fillets cut into strips
1 tablespoon of olive oil
100g broccoli florets
100g cauliflower florets

100g carrots cut into strips
100g celery cut into strips
1 onion, peeled and chopped
1 red pepper cut into strips
1 green pepper cut into strips
3 tablespoons of vegetable stock

**Method**: Heat the oil in a large non-stick pan or wok and add the chicken. Stir fry the chicken pieces until they are golden brown which will take approximately five minutes. Remove the chicken and add the vegetables to the pan with a little more oil if this is necessary to prevent them from sticking. When all the vegetables are tender add the chicken pieces again along with the stock, stir and cook for a further couple of minutes. Serve on a bed of rice or with noodles, chow mein or a pitta bread.

## Fruit cheesecake

**Ingredients**: 200g digestive biscuits crushed into crumbs
75g butter
Tinned fruit of your choice such as sliced peaches, mandarin segments, pear halves etc.
250g tub of mascarpone cheese
25g caster sugar

**Method**: Gently melt the butter over a low heat and add the biscuit crumbs. Mix well and then press into the base of cheesecake tin. Leave to cool in the fridge for about half an hour. Mix the cheese and sugar together and pour over the biscuit base and fruit. Smooth over and leave to chill. Strain the juice from the canned fruit and arrange on top of the cheesecake – serve immediately.

# Family meals

## Fish pie

**Ingredients**:

600g haddock or cod
6 large potatoes, peeled and cut into medium-sized chunks
200g broccoli florets
100g chopped celery
25g grated cheddar cheese

*For the sauce you will need:*
1 tablespoon of plain flour
500 ml semi-skimmed milk
100g grated cheddar cheesc

**Method**:

Bake the fish for about 20 minutes in a pre-heated oven set at 180°C/350°F/Gas Mark 4. Boil or steam the potatoes, drain and slice them into small discs about 5mm in thickness. Steam the remaining vegetables.

Make the cheese sauce by melting the butter in a saucepan and stirring in the flour. Gradually add the milk a little at a time stirring continuously and allowing the sauce to thicken. When all the milk has been added bring the sauce to a simmer, continuing to stir and add the cheese stirring until it is melted.

Flake the cooked fish into the bottom of a pie dish (removing any bones as you do so) and add the vegetables on top. Pour the cheese sauce over the fish and vegetables and arrange the potato disks evenly so that all the mixture is well covered. Sprinkle the top of the potatoes with the grated cheese and bake in the oven for 15 minutes or until the topping is golden brown. Serve with vegetables of your choice.

## Fresh fruit salad

**Ingredients**: A selection of at least five fruits which are in season. Try to opt for fruits of varying colours such as apples, pears, strawberries, blueberries, cherries, oranges, kiwi, mango, melon and pineapple.
6 tablespoons of fresh apple or orange juice (optional)

**Method**: Peel and chop the fruits as necessary removing any cores, pips or stones. Place in an attractive bowl and add the fruit juice. If you are using banana in your fruit salad don't add this until you are ready to serve as bananas go brown very quickly. Serve with fromage frais, crème fraiche, ice cream or fresh cream.

# Useful telephone numbers and websites

**Allergy UK** – 01322 619898 www.allergyuk.org.uk

**Asthma UK** – 08457 010203 www.asthma.org.uk

**Barnardo's** – 020 8550 8822 www.barnardos.org.uk

**British Dietetic Association** – 0121 200 8080 www.bda.uk.com

**Bullying UK** – 020 7378 1446 www.bullying.co.uk

**Child Accident Prevention Trust (CAPT)** – 020 7608 3828 www.capt.org.uk

**Childline** – 0800 1111 www.childline.co.uk

**Department of Health** – 020 7210 4850 www.doh.gov.uk

**Department for Children, Schools and Families (DCFS)** – 0845 60 222 60 www.teachernet.gov.uk

**Drugs helpline** – 0800 776600 www.talktofrank.com

**Eating Disorders Association** – 0845 634 7650 www.edauk.com

**Family Friends of Lesbian & Gays** – 01454 852 418 www.fflag.org.uk

**Family Planning** – 0845 310 1334 www.fpa.org.uk

**Family Rights Group** – 0800 731 1696 www.frg.org.uk

**Food Standards Agency** – 020 7276 8829 www.food.gov.uk

**Information for Teenagers about Sex and Relationships** – 0800 28 29 30 www.ruthinking.co.uk

**Internet Watch Hotline** – 0845 600 8844 www.iwf.org.uk

**Institute of Child Health** – 020 7242 9789 www.ich.ucl.ac.uk

**Kidscape** – 08451 205 204 www.kidscape.org.uk

**Message Home** – 0800 700 740 www.missingpeople.org.uk

**Missing Persons** – 0500 700 700 www.missingpersons.org

**National Children's Bureau** – 020 7843 6000 www.ncb.org.uk

**NHS Direct** – 0845 4647 www.nhsdirect.nhs.uk

**NSPCC** – 0808 800 5000 www.nspcc.org.uk

**Obesity Resource Information Centre** – 020 8503 2042 www.aso.org.uk

**Parentline Plus** – 020 7284 5500 www.parentlineplus.org.uk

**Relate** – 0300 100 1234 www.relate.org.uk

**Royal Society for the Prevention of Accidents (RoSPA)** – 0121 248 2000 www.rospa.com

**Samaritans** – 0845 790 9090 www.smaritans.org

**Save the Children** – 020 7703 5400 www.savethechildren.org.uk

**Shelter** – 0800 446441 www.shelter.org.uk

**Smokers Quitline** – 0800 002200 www.quit.org.uk

**Vegetarian Society** – 0161 925 2000 www.vegsoc.org

**Victim Support** – 01702 333 911 www.victimsupport.org.uk

# Index

**A**

action rhymes, 144
active games, 145
additives 136, 216-17
adolescence, 192
adoptive family, 23
alcohol, 135
allergies
  egg, 206-7
  milk, 204-6
  preventing, 204
  wheat, 206
anaphylactic shock, 203-4
anorexia nervosa, 197-8
anxiousness, 40
appetite, 237
assertiveness, 113-19
associative play, 93
attention seeking, 41
authoritarian parents, 8, 11
authoritative parents, 8, 10

**B**

baby blues, 33
behaviour
  changes in, 112
  influences on, 38, 45-6
  learning, 43-4
  unacceptable, 37
belonging, 67
body image, 196
body language, 75-6
Body Mass Index, 230-1
boredom, 38-9
bottle feeding, 167-8
boundaries, 9, 43, 50-1
breakfast, 140, 150-1, 193
breastfeeding, 166-7
bully, 107-11
bullying
  components of, 106-7
  dealing with, 115-17
  recognising, 113
  signs, 113-15
  understanding, 115

**C**

cafes *see* restaurants
calcium, 133, 266
calories, 176, 188-9, 192-3
comfort eating, 226
carbohydrates, 127-8

chickenpox, 210
choices, 68
colds, 210
confidence, 90
confusion, 42
constipation, 212
control, 89-90
co-operative play, 94
couch potatoes, 141
counselling, 105
cow's milk, 168-9
culture, 34-5
cycling, 190-1

**D**
dance, 144
death, 32
dehydration, 212-13
diarrhoea, 212, 214
diet, 24-9, 173
disability, 36
distraction, 80
divorce, 29-32
drama, 144

**E**
emotions, 42, 100-2
empowerment, 67-8
exercise, 195-6
  dangerous, 200-1
  encouraging, 234
energy, 264-5
expectations, 52
extended family, 21-2
eye contact, 78

**F**
facial expressions, 78
falling out, 95, 99-100
family life, 3, 72
fast food, 223-4
fathers, 18
fats, 26-7, 129-30, 221-2
feelings
  accepting, 82, 85
  denying, 83-5
  overwhelming, 86-7
  showing, 85
  understanding, 82
fibre, 135, 265
fine motor skills,143
finger foods, 173-4, 178
five-a-day, 151, 225-7
fizzy drinks, 222
food
  allergies, 202-3
  intolerances, 202
  labels, 27, 153-5
  poisoning, 161-3
  preparation, 160-1
  pyramid, 125
  safety, 157-8
  storage 159-60
formula milk, 167-8
foster family, 23
frameworks, 62-4
friendships, 92, 95, 98
fruit, 138
frustration, 40
fussy eaters, 155, 176

G
gay family, 22
gender ,36
gross motor skills, 143
growth rate, 175, 189

H
habits, 177
hand washing, 163-4
harmful foods, 172
house rules, 62-4
humiliation, 79

I
illness, 34, 39
impetigo, 210
independence, 179
individuality, 91
influenza, 210-11
iron, 133-4, 266
isolation, 76

L
learning difficulties,43
lesbian family, 22
lunch boxes, 249-54

M
measles, 211
medication, 214-15
minerals, 133
mixed ethnic family, 23
motivation, 65-7
motor skills, 143
moving house, 35

N
nomadic family, 23
nuclear family, 21
nutrients, 126-7
nutrition
  3-5 year olds, 182-3
  babies, 165-6
  differences in, 193-4
  school age, 188-9
  teenagers, 192-3
  toddlers, 176-7
  when ill, 209

O
obstacle course
  indoor, 145
  outdoor, 146
OFSTED, 245
Oliver, Jamie, 244
organic food, 241-3
outdoor exercise, 146-7, 184-6

P
pacing, 143
parallel play, 93
parental conflict, 70
parental influence, 12-13
park, 59
permissive parents, 8-9
physical exercise, 141
  benefits of, 142
  obstacles to, 147-8
play therapy, 80-1
popularity, 95-6
portions, 152, 238

potential, 67
preferences, eating, 177, 236
pressure, 6
proteins, 129, 265
public transport, 59
punishments, 76, 112

**Q**
quality time, 5-6

**R**
recipes
  0-12 months, 269-72
  0-3 years, 272-3
  3-5 years, 273-4
  5-12 years, 274-5
  families, 277-8
  teenagers, 275-6
reconstituted family, 22-3
respect, 48-9
  gaining, 50-1
  showing, 48, 50, 66
responsibility, 6, 68, 90
restaurants, 56-7
restriction, 178
rewards, 69-70
role models, 3-4, 12, 14, 55, 92, 197, 235-6
routine, 51
rules, 47-8, 64

**S**
safety, 66
  playground, 184-5
safety zones, 51
salt, 219-20
sanctions, 77-9
schools
  changing, 119-20
  meals, 244-8
self concept, 85-6
self respect, 54-5, 89
shopping, 152-3
shouting, 74
shyness, 13, 103-4
siblings, 13, 32-3
single parents, 19-20, 22
skills, toddlers, 180-1
smacking, 72-4
snacking, 225, 227-9
social acceptance, 54, 97
solitary play, 93
spectator play, 93
sport, 190
stickers, 70
stomach complaints, 211
sugar, 218-19
supermarket, 58-9
support, 87
sweets, 70

**T**
table manners, 57-8, 182-3
takeaways, 222-3
tantrums, 55, 60-1
television, 181
temper, 13
temperament, 71
timeout, 79
tiredness, 39
tofu, 267
tonsillitis, 211

toys, 70
traffic light system, 154
triggers, 72

**U**

unemployment, 35-6

**V**

vegetables,138
vegetarian diet, 262-8
victim, 112-13
vitamins, 26, 130-3, 266
vomiting, 22, 214

**W**

walking, 190-1
water, 135, 140
weaning, 169-71
working parents, 4-5

**Z**

zinc, 267